14.99

FAST CARDS

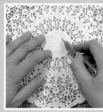

FAST **CARDS**

Techniques and projects for producing greetings cards – quickly

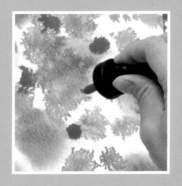

S A R A H   B E A M A N

COLLINS & BROWN

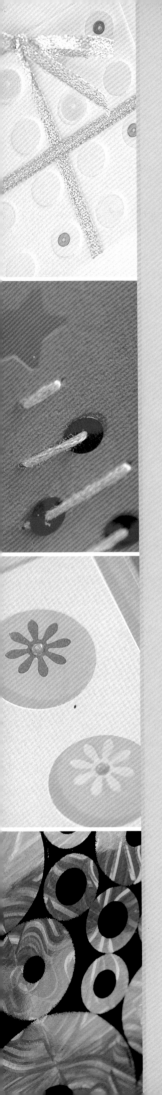

To Kate;

for opportunity, advice and much merriment.

Thank you. X

First published in Great Britain in 2004
by Collins & Brown Limited
The Chrysalis Building
Bramley Road
London W10 6SP

An imprint of **Chrysalis** Books Group plc

9 8 7 6 5 4 3 2

British Library Cataloguing-in-Publication Data:
A catalogue record for this book is available from the British Library.

ISBN 1 84340 151 7

Conceived, edited and designed by Collins & Brown Limited

Editor: Kate Haxell
Designer: Justina Leitão
Photography: Matthew Dickens

Reproduction by Classicscan
Printed and bound in Malaysia by Times

Distributed in the United States and Canada by
Sterling Publishing Co.
387 Park Avenue South, New York, NY 10016, USA

contents

CLARE
&
DAVID

introduction

Most of us send a large number of greetings cards each year, usually shop-bought ones that can be both expensive and a little impersonal. Though the array of commercial cards is considerably more inventive than it once was, there is nothing better than a card that has been made for its recipient with love and care. However, while it might be satisfying and pleasurable to create unique hand-made cards, our busy lives sometimes prevent this.

This book includes a range of techniques and projects designed to overcome the limitations of time and deliver the special greeting that a hand-made card reflects. Some simple equipment and a few basic materials stored in an accessible place mean you will always be prepared, though there are some more specialised bits of kit that are worth investing in for their practicality and versatility (see *Materials & equipment*, page 10).

The first chapter of the book offers basic techniques that will stand you in good stead for most card-making projects. Simple to do and using basic materials, they illustrate how easy it can be to decorate a card. The second chapter contains techniques and projects made from household items, as well as widely available craft materials, and illustrates how they can be used to make effective cards, fast. Especially useful when an important birthday has slipped your mind and you need to catch the post, or worse still, you realize it's your wedding anniversary! These projects should help you to avoid any such embarrassments.

There are occasions when it would be lovely to send out hand-made cards, but the quantity you need seems to make this prohibitive – a wedding invitation, for example. The final chapter of the book looks at making cards in quantities. There are techniques for using and adapting printed images, mass-producing motifs, adding text and decorating paper. From small batches of cards to larger production runs, the projects illustrated are not only fun to do, but will guarantee a unique and personal greeting that often works out to be more economical than the shop-bought alternative, too. Happy card making!

Sarah Beaman

getting started

In this chapter you will find advice on the tools and equipment you will need to make your cards. Many items you may well already have at home and others are widely available from craft stores. Also in this chapter are a number of basic making and decorating techniques – from folding your own cards and attaching different motifs to simple decorating techniques – that will be useful for many of the cards you make.

materials & equipment

SHOWN HERE ARE THE
BASIC TOOLS YOU WILL
NEED TO MAKE MOST
CARDS, SO READ THESE
PAGES AND DECIDE ON
WHAT TO INVEST IN TO
START WITH: YOU CAN BUY
MORE EQUIPMENT AS YOU
NEED IT. HOWEVER, IT IS
WORTH CHECKING THAT
YOU HAVE WHAT YOU NEED
TO MAKE A PARTICULAR
PROJECT BEFORE YOU
START. THERE IS LITTLE
MORE IRRITATING THAN
HAVING TO STOP HALFWAY,
OR MAKING A MESS OF A
CARD BECAUSE YOU DON'T
HAVE THE ITEM YOU NEED.

Drawing

✪ A putty rubber that can be moulded to a point to rub out tiny marks.

✪ A soft pencil so you can rub out marks easily.

Cutting

✪ A self-healing cutting mat with the measurement system you prefer.

✪ A steel rule with the measurement system you prefer.

✪ A craft knife with a retractable blade for safety.

✪ Scissors with sharp points for cutting out detail.

✪ A bone folder, for scoring card before folding it.

Sticking

✪ Paper adhesive, the kind that comes in a stick is good.

✪ All-purpose adhesive, the gel-type is least messy.

✪ A glue pen, for sticking small items.

✪ Spray glue, good for sticking thin paper and delicate items.

✪ Fabric glue, for sticking most types of fabric and ribbon.

✪ Self-adhesive pads, for raising items off the surface of a card.

✪ A brayer, for rolling over glued items to ensure that they are flat and firmly stuck.

✪ Double-sided tape, very useful for sticking all sorts of items to cards, available in various widths.

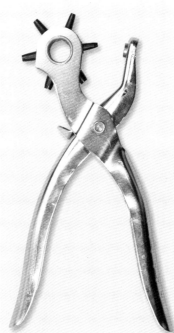

Paper and card

✪ Keep an assortment of coloured cardstock and papers, plus pre-scored card blanks and aperture cards.

Stamping

✪ Rubber stamps are available in an enormous range of designs and sizes.

✪ Ink pads come in many different colours and finishes and have several different uses.

Punching

✪ A leather punch can be used to produce different-sized holes.

✪ Hobby punches come in many shapes and sizes and have many applications.

Decorating

✪ Vari-coloured machine embroidery thread makes simple stitching more attractive. Look out for vari-coloured hand embroidery threads as well.

✪ Sequins in different shapes and colours are versatile and can add instant decorative detail.

✪ Lengths of ribbon and scraps of fabrics will always come in useful.

Colouring

✪ Inks can be bought in a range of colours. You can also use watercolour paints to colour cards.

✪ Buy inexpensive paintbrushes in a range of widths and bristle stiffness.

folding a card

Pre-scored and folded card blanks are widely available in a range of sizes, finishes and colours. However, there are times when it is necessary or desirable to make your own card blank, so having a variety of cardstock stored away means you can make a card at a moment's notice.

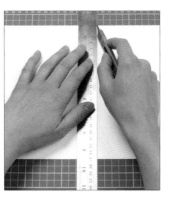  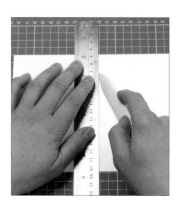

1 Using a steel rule and craft knife on a cutting mat, cut the card to the size you want it to be when opened out flat.

2 Using a pencil and the rule, establish the middle and make a tiny mark at the top and bottom of the card.

3 Lay the rule between the pencil marks and score along it with a bone folder. Bone folders are available in craft stores, but if you don't have one, the back of a table knife will do just as well.

SCORING CARD

Whether you score on the inside or outside of the card depends on the type of card you are using. Some types of card 'feather' along the scored line when folded, so these are best scored on the inside. Experiment on a scrap piece before scoring the actual card.

4 Fold the card along the scored line, creasing it firmly.

double-sided tape

This is a convenient, versatile and mess-free sticking medium. Invest in a narrow and a wider tape; you can always trim down wide tape as required. Invisible mounts are small pre-cut pieces of double-sided tape and provide a quick and easy option for some applications.

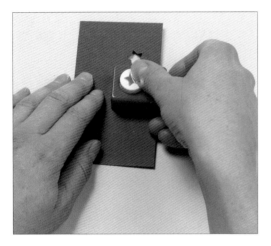

1 Using a hobby punch, punch a row of stars in a piece of paper (see *Punching shapes*, page 20). Cut the punched paper to the size you want.

2 Stick lengths of double-sided tape along the edges of the back of the paper.

PUNCHED SHAPES

Save the punched-out shapes for decorating future cards. They can be stuck to a card with paper adhesive (see Adhesives, page 16) or self-adhesive pads (see Self-adhesive pads, page 18).

3 Peel the backing off the tape.

4 Position the paper over the card and lay it down. Smooth over the taped edges to ensure that they are firmly stuck.

double-sided film

With the same attributes as double-sided tape, double-sided film comes in sheet form in a range of sizes, making it especially useful in applications where tape is too narrow. Try cutting it with decorative scissors, using it to stick down larger motifs or to bond fabric to card.

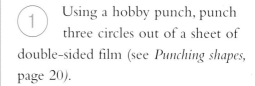

(1) Using a hobby punch, punch three circles out of a sheet of double-sided film (see *Punching shapes,* page 20).

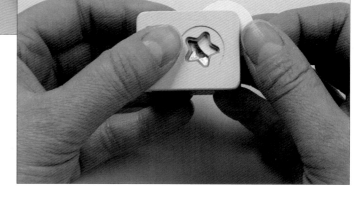

(2) Turn a star hobby punch upside down so that you can see where you are punching. Slide each circle into the punch and punch out a star.

(3) Peel the backing off one side of the circles of film.

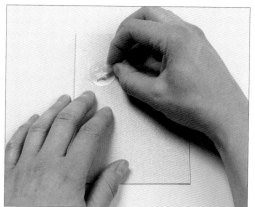

(4) Stick the circles onto the card, arranging them as you wish.

(5) Peel the remaining backing off just one of the circles to reveal the sticky film.

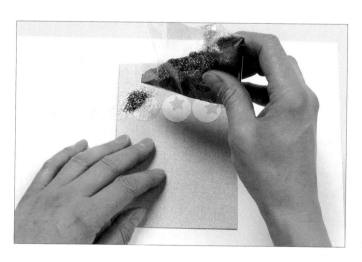

(6) Lay the card on a sheet of scrap paper to catch the glitter. Sprinkle one colour of glitter over the film, making sure all of the sticky surface is covered. Pat the glitter with your finger to ensure that it is firmly stuck.

PEELING

Never try to peel both backings off the film before you stick it to the card. The film is thin and tears quite easily, and it is very sticky so it will immediately try to stick to itself.

(7) Tip the excess glitter off onto the scrap paper. Fold the paper into a scoop and pour the glitter back into the pot to be used again.

(8) Repeat the process with each circle. Peeling off one covering at a time allows you to make each circle a different colour.

adhesives

Adhesive should never be visible on a card so choose the right type for a professional result. The driest kind possible that is also suitable for the material you are working with is usually best. If you are using different materials on a single card you will need a variety of appropriate adhesives.

(1) A good paper adhesive for card–making is the stick kind: liquid glues can spread and be messy. Apply the adhesive over the back of the paper, ensuring that the edges are coated. It is best to lay the paper on a scrap piece so that you can glue right over the edges. Be careful not to crease the paper.

(2) Position one end of the glued paper exactly where you want it to be, aligning any straight edges carefully and accurately. Then smooth the rest of the paper down across the card.

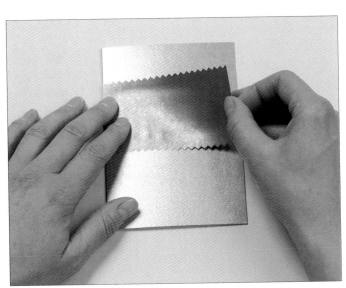

③ To neaten the ends of a piece of wire-edged ribbon, lay the ribbon right-side down on the card. Lay a ruler along the edge of the card and fold the ribbon over it. Do the same at the other end to make the length of ribbon the same width as the card with the cut edges folded under out of sight.

④ Spread a little fabric glue over the back of the ribbon and stick the folded ends down, then spread more glue on the folded ends. If the ribbon – or fabric – is thin, test the glue on a scrap piece first to ensure that it doesn't soak through to the front. If it does, try using double-sided tape.

You will often need adhesive of some sort or another so keep a selection together in a drawer, then they are always there for a last-minute card. As well as the types shown here, spray glue is a useful investment for gluing fine or delicate items. Always use it in a well-ventilated room. Another useful tool is a glue pen for sticking tiny items, such as sequins or 'gems'.

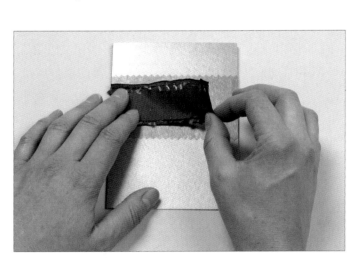

⑤ Position one end of the glued ribbon on the card exactly where you want it to be, aligning any straight edges carefully and accurately. Then lay the rest of the ribbon down and gently pat it in place.

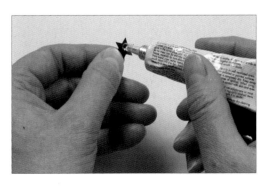

⑥ Dab a spot of all-purpose glue on the back of a sequin.

⑦ Lightly press the sequin in place. Leave the card to dry.

self-adhesive pads

These pads come in a variety of sizes and thicknesses, from tiny dots to chunky squares and are used to create relief effects. Foam tape is also available and offers great creative flexibility as it can be used as a continuous adhesive strip or be cut to fit the required size or shape.

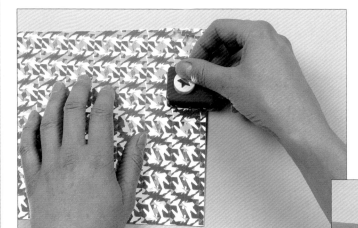

① Using a hobby punch, punch out a number of stars from holographic paper (see *Punching shapes*, page 20).

② Stick a small self-adhesive pad to the back of each star.

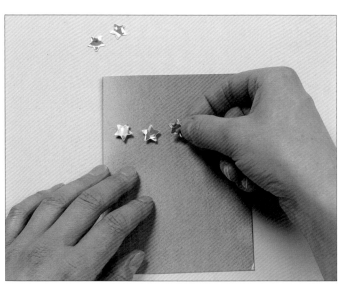

③ Peel the backing off each pad and stick the stars onto the card.

PUNCHING SHAPES

When you are punching out shapes, punch them out in neat lines or patterns and save the piece of punched paper to use as a panel to decorate another card.

paper fasteners

Paper fasteners, or brads, offer a mess-free fixing method. In addition to the brass type used in offices, look out for mini brads in an exciting range of colours from specialist craft and hobby stores. The scale of these makes them particularly attractive and useful for card making.

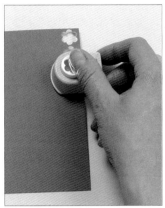

1 Using a hobby punch, punch flowers out of different-coloured papers (see *Punching shapes*, page 20).

2 Carefully cut a tiny slit in the centre of each flower with a craft knife. The slit must be just wide enough for the legs of a paper fastener to pass through.

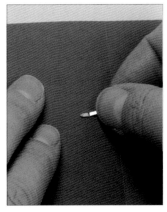

3 Open the card out flat and cut a matching slit in the front, where you want the flower to be.

4 Pass a paper fastener through the slit in the flower, then through a slit in the front of the card.

5 Turn the card over and open out the fastener's legs. Repeat until all the flowers are attached.

MOVEMENT

If you punch a hole in the motif and cut a slit in the card, the motif will be able to spin on the paper fastener. This simple form of movement can add an extra dimension to a card.

punching shapes

As well as the office file punch, a wide variety of hobby punches are available and they can be used in many ways. Both the punched motif and the hole it creates are valuable, allowing you to play with positive and negative shapes and easily create a number of cards at the same time.

FILE
PUNCHES

Remember to empty the file punch before you start so that you can see and save the punched circles easily.

①   Stick a piece of double-sided film to the back of a piece of coloured paper (see *Double-sided film*, page 14).

②   Using a file punch, punch out some circles, spacing them widely on the paper. Save the punched-out circles.

③   Turn a flower hobby punch upside down and slide the paper into it, positioning it so that one of the punched holes is in the centre of the flower. Punch out a flower; you will have to press hard on the punch to punch through the paper and double-sided film. Punch out as many flowers as you need.

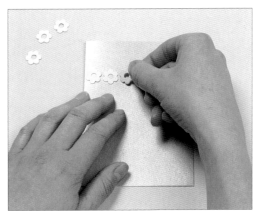

④ Slide the paper into an upside-down circle punch, positioning it so that a flower is within the circle, though not necessarily in the middle. Punch out as many circles as you need.

⑤ Make one card by peeling the backing off the flowers and sticking them to the card.

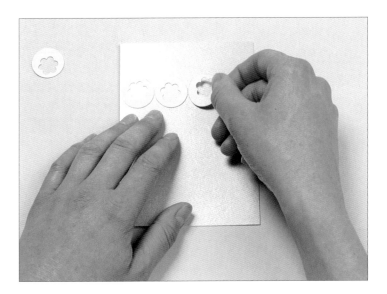

⑥ Make a second card by peeling off the backing and sticking the circles onto the card.

⑦ Complete the second card by sticking the circles saved from Step 2 into the middles of the larger circles.

punching apertures

An aperture in the front of a card is an attractive way of framing a motif. Pre-cut aperture cards are available, but you can cut your own or, quicker still, use a paper punch. This looks most effective on duplex card, where a contrast colour shows through the aperture.

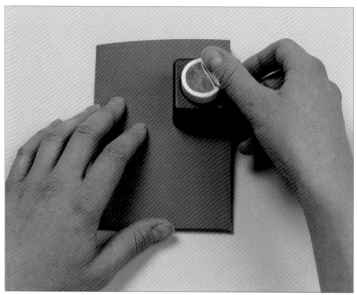

① Using a circular hobby punch, punch an aperture in the front of a card.

DUPLEX CARD

Available from good stationers and hobby stores, duplex card is a single piece of card made up of two colours laminated together. You could achieve a similar, though not as speedy, effect by sticking a contrasting internal leaf inside the card (see Internal leaf, page 88).

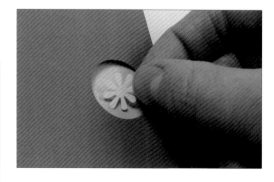

② Put a dot of all-purpose adhesive (see *Adhesives*, page 16) on the back of a sequin. With the card closed, stick the sequin to the inside back of the card, centring it carefully in the punched-out circle.

machine-stitching

Simple machine stitches provide an alternative method of attaching thin items to a card face and don't require a high level of sewing skill. Coloured thread can give bolder decorative detail, though here invisible thread is used to complement the translucent quality of the sequins.

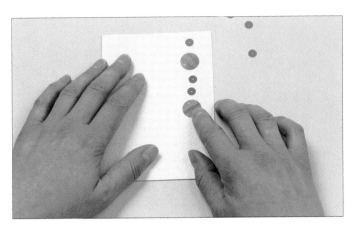

1   Arrange the sequins on the card. It is simplest to sew them on in a straight line.

TESTING STITCHES

Always test the machine-stitch on some spare card, as any mistakes will be clearly visible. If the stitch length is too small you will over-perforate the card and it may fall apart.

2   Using invisible thread in the sewing machine, stitch a straight line right down the front of the card, stitching over the sequins. Stitch slowly and carefully, making sure that none of the sequins slip.

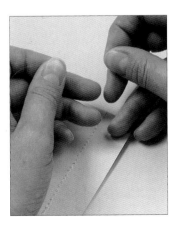

3   Tie the loose ends of the threads in a double knot and trim them short.

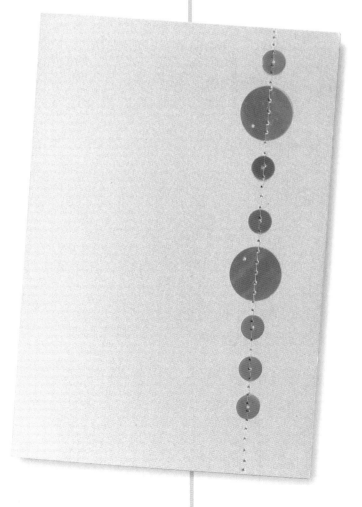

spraying

Spraying over items placed on a card can produce great silhouettes, so look out for items with attractive outlines. You may need to use low-tack spray adhesive to hold the item in position while you spray, though here self-adhesive hole-reinforcers are used to create a simple design.

① Mask off the back of an opened-out card with paper and low-tack masking tape. Stick the tape along the score line so that only the front of the card will be coloured.

② Stick hole reinforcers in a pattern on the front of the card. To make the reinforcers low-tack, stick them to a piece of fabric and peel them off, then stick them to the card.

③ Place the card on a piece of scrap paper and spray over it with enamel paint. Leave the paint to dry until it is just tacky.

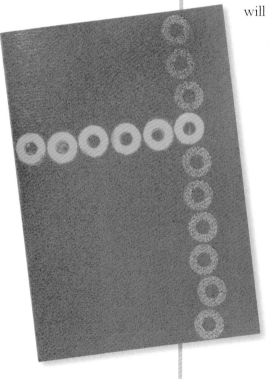

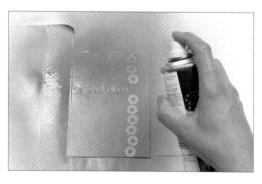

④ Working carefully without touching the paint on the card, use a craft knife to lift the edge of some of the reinforcers. Peel them off.

⑤ Spray over the card again with glitter spray paint. Leave to dry until tacky, and then remove the remaining reinforcers, as in Step 4. Peel off the masking tape and remove the paper. Leave to dry completely.

found objects

This technique can lead to some surprising and effective results, and there is no shortage of items worth experimenting with. As with other printing techniques, there is the advantage of being able to reproduce the motif easily and quickly as many times as you want.

① Press the object, here a star-shaped cookie cutter, onto an ink pad. Ensure that all the surfaces you want to print with are covered with ink.

② Press the cutter onto the card. Press firmly to transfer as much ink as possible.

③ Lift the cutter cleanly off the card to reveal the printed image. The outline may be slightly broken, but this is part of the hand-printed effect.

④ Cookie cutters often come in different-sized sets; here a set of three was used to print concentric stars. Leave the card to dry after printing it.

CLEANING OBJECTS

If you are using objects to print with that are usually used with food – like these cookie cutters – remember to wash them thoroughly after printing.

potato printing

A staple cooking ingredient that most of us will have to hand, the potato should not be overlooked as a medium for making a quick and simple stamp. This method ensures a more sophisticated outcome than some of those rather naïve schooldays' results.

1 Cut a large potato in half lengthwise. Press a round cookie cutter into the surface, pushing it approximately 1cm (½in) down into the potato flesh.

2 Using a small, sharp knife, cut away all the potato around the outer edge of the cutter. Cut to a depth of approximately 1cm (½in). Always be careful doing this and never cut towards your hand.

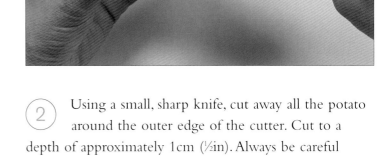

3 Pull the cutter off the potato to reveal the raised shape.

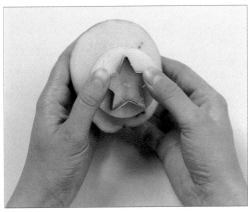

4   Press a star-shaped cutter into the cut-out circle, again pressing it in approximately 1cm (½in).

5   Cut out the potato inside the star, cutting up to the inside edge of the cookie cutter. Cut to a depth of approximately 1cm (½in).

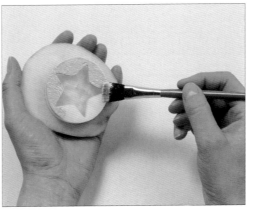

6   Remove the star cutter. Lay the potato face-down on some kitchen paper for a few minutes to absorb any excess moisture.

7   Using a soft paintbrush, brush emulsion paint onto the raised surface of the potato. Ensure that the whole raised area is painted.

SHAPED CUTTERS

You can also simply press a cookie cutter into a potato and cut away the excess to make a shaped stamp.

8   Press the potato down onto the card. Lift it off cleanly to reveal the printed image. Wipe any remaining paint off the potato with kitchen towel and repeat the process with a different-coloured paint.

stencilling

Stencils can be used with a variety of techniques to produce a repeated motif or design. This technique utilizes an ink pad, which is quite dry so the colour is less likely to seep under the stencil. Applying the colour with a cotton bud means you can be quite precise, even on small motifs.

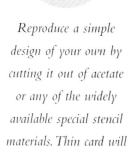

MAKING A
STENCIL

Reproduce a simple design of your own by cutting it out of acetate or any of the widely available special stencil materials. Thin card will be fine if you are only planning on using the stencil a few times.

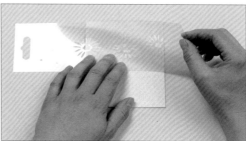

① Spray the back of a stencil with low-tack spray glue.

② Position the stencil on a card and press it down firmly.

③ Dab the tip of a cotton bud onto an ink pad to pick up a little ink. Dab the ink onto the stencil to colour sections of it in.

④ It is quite easy to achieve shaded effects by using different colours on the same sections of the stencil. Use a clean cotton bud tip for each new colour.

⑤ Carefully peel the stencil off the card to reveal the design. Leave to dry.

stamping

Using a purchased rubber stamp is an easy way to make a professional-looking card in double-quick time. As with hobby punches, one or two carefully selected motifs will make a worthwhile investment as they are very versatile and can be used in a variety of creative applications.

INK
PADS

These are widely available in a huge range of colours and types. It is well worth buying a couple in your favourite colours as they have several uses in card making.

① Press a rubber stamp onto a rainbow ink pad, positioning the stamp so that it picks up two of the colours.

② Stamp onto the card. Repeat the process, ensuring that you press the stamp onto the pad in the same place each time to avoid mixing the ink colours.

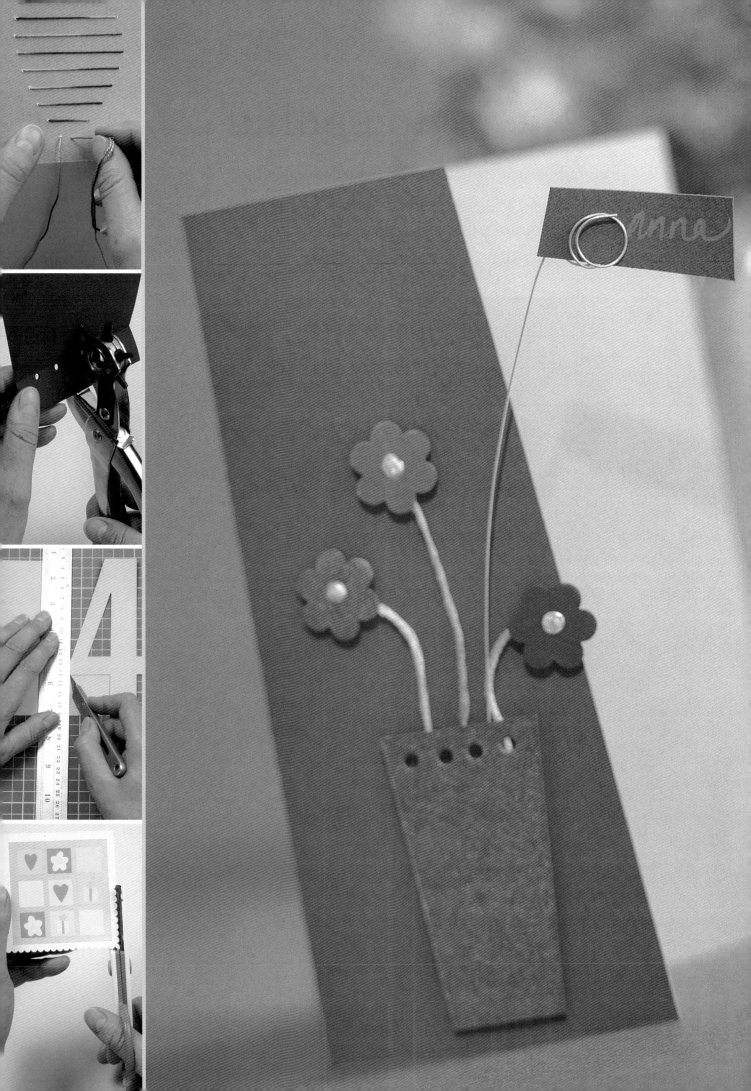

last-minute cards

All of us have, at one time or another, suddenly realized that tomorrow is a friend's birthday and that the last post is in half-an-hour. There isn't time to go out and buy a card, but some quick work can save the day. The first section of this chapter looks at single techniques, which in themselves can be used to create simple yet stunning cards. The second section shows you how to combine techniques to produce more complex cards – perfect if you have just a little more time.

simple shaped card

A single-fold card can easily be transformed with a few simple cuts. The new silhouette can form the design in its own right, or time permitting, be embellished further. With a little imagination this template could be adapted to make a beach hut, a circus tent or a puppet theatre.

ALL OF THE TECHNIQUES IN THIS SECTION CONCENTRATE ON MAKING SINGLE CARDS, QUICKLY, FROM ITEMS YOU ARE LIKELY TO HAVE TO HAND – PIECES OF COLOURED PAPER AND CARD, SCRAPS OF RIBBON AND FABRIC, LEAVES AND FLOWERS FROM THE GARDEN AND HOUSEHOLD ITEMS LIKE KITCHEN FOIL AND STRING. NOTHING TAKES LONGER THAN HALF-AN-HOUR AND MANY CAN BE COMPLETED IN MINUTES.

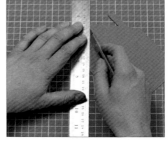

1 Trace off the template on page 123 and transfer it onto the front of the card.

2 Using a craft knife and steel rule on a cutting mat, and with the card folded, cut out the outline shape.

3 Open the card out and cut out the windows. Cut along the top and down the right-hand side of the door.

4 Using a bone folder, score down the left-hand side of the door. Crease the card along this score line so that the door can be opened and closed.

5 Give the window in the door a rounded top with a small circular punch. Position the punch so that it sits halfway over the cut edge and punch out a half-circle (see *Punching shapes*, page 20). Use a leather punch to make a small hole for the door handle.

simple pop-up card

Quick to create and very adaptable, this is a fun method of presenting a motif, since it will rise up from the surface of the card when it is opened. The position and length of the tab can be adjusted to suit the card and the motif you wish to use.

① Lay the pop-up – here a gift-wrap motif (see *Gift wrap*, page 39) – on the front of a closed card, positioning it where you would like it to be inside the card. To establish the length of the tab, measure from the fold to a point halfway across the motif and mark this point on the front of the card.

② Draw two horizontal, parallel pencil lines, about 1cm (½in) apart, from the fold to the marked point.

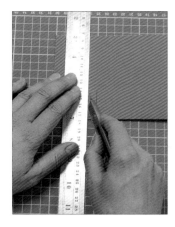

③ With the card folded and using a steel rule and craft knife on a cutting mat, cut along the pencil lines.

④ Open the card out and gently push the cut-out tab in. If the card is thick you may need to score across the ends of the lines to make it fold in. Close the card so the tab is on the inside.

⑤ Using paper adhesive (see *Adhesives*, page 16), stick the pop-up piece to the front of the tab.

POP-UPS

Anything lightweight can be used for the pop-up: a photograph, an image from a magazine or a section of patterned gift wrap all work well. If the pop-up is not stiff enough, mount it on a piece of card first.

ribbon

A small stock of ribbons of various types and widths will be useful in all kinds of card-making projects. Look out for interesting colours and designs and buy a short length when you see them. Here, ribbon provides the decoration on a card suitable for a number of occasions.

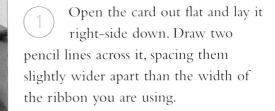

1   Open the card out flat and lay it right-side down. Draw two pencil lines across it, spacing them slightly wider apart than the width of the ribbon you are using.

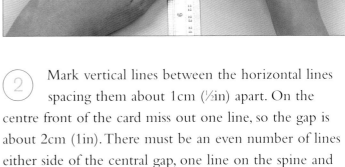

2   Mark vertical lines between the horizontal lines spacing them about 1cm (½in) apart. On the centre front of the card miss out one line, so the gap is about 2cm (1in). There must be an even number of lines either side of the central gap, one line on the spine and an uneven number across the back of the card.

3   Using a craft knife and steel rule on a cutting mat, cut along the vertical lines. Ensure that the cuts stop at the top and bottom horizontal lines.

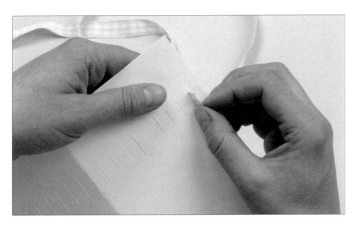

④ Stick a small strip of double-sided tape (see *Double-sided tape*, page 13) to each outer front edge of the card. The strip of tape must be shorter than the cut slits and sit between the last slit and the edge of the card. Working from the back, thread one end of a piece of ribbon through the last slit on the front and stick the end to the tape.

⑤ Bring the long free end of the ribbon around from the back of the card and thread it down through the same slit, covering the stuck-down end.

RIBBON

You can embellish the card further by hanging a decorative item from the bow. A tiny tassel, a string of beads or a drilled shell all work well. This is also a pretty way to present a gift of a pendant.

⑥ Weave the ribbon in and out of the slits until you reach the central gap, where it should be on the right side. Cut the ribbon off, leaving a tail about 30cm (12in) long.

⑦ Repeat the process from the other side of the card, weaving the ribbon in and out through the slits on the back and spine of the card, and then through the slits on the front. When you reach the central gap, cut the ribbon off, leaving a tail as before.

⑧ Tie the two ends of the ribbon in a neat bow on the front of the card. Trim the ends so that they slope in opposite directions.

hand-stitching

There is no need to consider stitch solely in conjunction with cloth, as many techniques transfer well onto paper and can offer the card maker a wealth of interesting and unusual possibilities. These very simple stitches could easily be embellished with beads, sequins or charms.

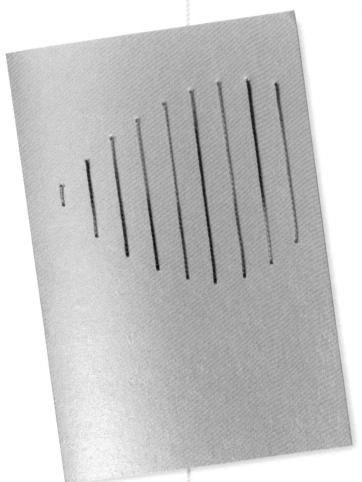

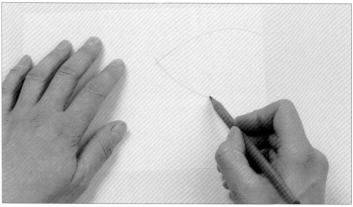

① Cut tracing paper to the size of the front of a card. Either trace off the template on page 124, or draw your own shape onto the tracing paper.

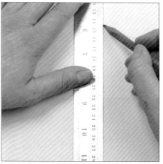

② If you have drawn your own shape, make pencil marks at 1cm (½in) intervals along the drawn lines. The marks should be opposite one another.

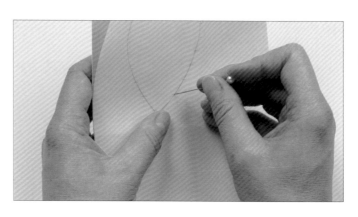

③ With the card open, lay the tracing paper over the front of it and use a pin to pierce holes at each marked point. Remove the tracing paper.

④ Thread a needle with a long length of embroidery thread and tie a knot in one end. Working from the back, push the needle through the hole nearest the edge of the card and pull the thread through right up to the knot.

⑤ Push the needle through the hole opposite the one you came out of to make a long stitch. Bring the needle up through the next hole along.

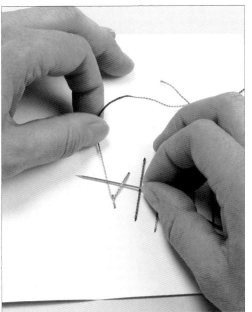

⑥ Repeat the process until you have made all the stitches.

⑦ Fasten off the end of the thread on the inside of the card by looping it around an adjacent stitch and knotting it tightly.

EMBROIDERY THREAD

For simple but effective results, look out for vari-coloured embroidery threads, like the type used here.

seeds

An attractive packet containing a few leftover seeds can decorate a card to please a green-fingered friend. You could try making the card from hand-made paper with flower inclusions, or incorporating different seeds on the same card as they do have interesting and variable forms.

PACKAGING

Many foods have attractive packaging or labels that can be recycled to make cards, so save interesting pieces as you see them.

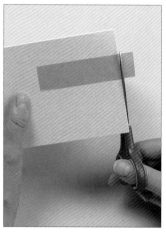

① Cut a length of double-sided tape and stick it on the card with one end protruding over the front edge.

② Using scissors, trim the tape flush with the edge of the card. Peel the paper backing off the tape.

③ Cut a piece of a pretty seed packet to the same depth and approximately two-thirds of the length of the tape. Stick this to the left-hand end of the tape, aligning the edges carefully.

④ Lay the card on a piece of scrap paper and sprinkle flower seeds over the exposed tape. Pat the seeds down with your finger.

⑤ Tip off the excess seeds onto the scrap paper.

gift wrap

Gift-wrap, new or used, is an easy way to add an image to a card and can provide a co-ordinated look if a gift is wrapped with the remaining paper. Store suitable pieces of wrap and two potential problems can be resolved at once. Consider making a matching gift tag, too.

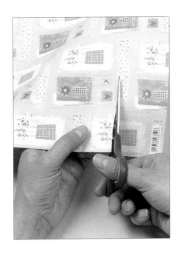 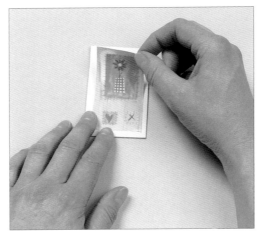 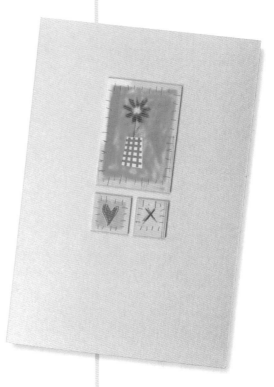

① Using scissors, roughly cut out the piece of the gift wrap that you would like to use on your card.

② Spray glue (see *Adhesives*, page 16) over the back of the gift wrap and stick it to a slightly larger piece of thick cardboard. This will give the motif a slight relief effect.

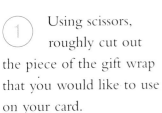   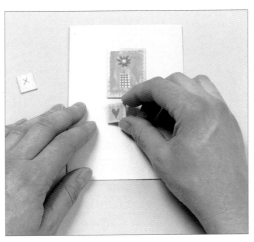

③ Using a craft knife and steel ruler on a cutting mat, cut out the sections of gift wrap accurately.

④ Apply paper adhesive to the back of the cardboard and stick the pieces of mounted gift wrap to the card.

GIFT WRAP

The best gift wrap to use with this technique is one that has a small pattern within simple shapes, such as squares or circles. These are easy to cut out neatly and are usually the right scale.

kitchen foil

Aluminium foil can be found in most store cupboards and although it can be flimsy, it becomes a viable medium for embossing techniques once mounted onto thin card. The end result can be quite ornate, giving little clue to its modest origin.

① Cut a sheet of thin card slightly larger than the panel you want. Stick a piece of double-sided film (see *Double-sided film*, page 14) to it and peel off the backing. Stick a piece of kitchen foil to the film, being careful not to wrinkle it.

② Lay the foil panel on two sheets of kitchen paper, then lay a photocopy of the motif on page 124 over the foil. Draw over the motif with an embossing tool. Press firmly to emboss the lines into the foil. Remove the photocopy.

★ EMBOSSING TOOL

If you don't have an embossing tool, you can use a dried-up ballpoint pen instead.

③ Leaving a plain, narrow border around the edge, cut out the motif with decorative-edge scissors.

④ Use the embossing tool to embellish the scalloped edge with curls and dots. Do not press too hard or you will tear the foil. Where necessary, draw over the lines of the motif again to strengthen them.

⑤ Stick a self-adhesive pad to each corner of the back of the foil, and one in the middle (see *Self-adhesive pads*, page 18). Stick the motif to a card.

wire

This is a good presentation technique for pendants, Christmas decorations, and other trinkets or mementos, as they can be removed and used by the recipient. For extra ornament, you could thread small beads onto the craft wire before you coil it.

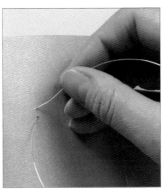

1 Position the pendant on the card. Using a pin, pierce two holes in the front of the card, one through the hole in the pendant and the other just above the first one.

2 Cut approximately 50cm (20in) of craft wire. Working from the back of the card, poke one end of the wire through each hole.

WIRE

3 Thread the pendant onto the lower piece of wire and push it right up to the card. Twist the wires tightly together.

4 Wind one end of the wire around a pencil to make a coil. Slide the wire coil off the pencil. Repeat the process with the other end.

5 Press the coils flat with your fingers.

Craft wire is available in a number of different colours and finishes. You can also use thick fuse wire for this technique.

baking parchment

Ordinary baking parchment can be used to create an attractive card when there is little else to hand. This technique, though of Japanese origin, is reminiscent of schooldays' paper-cutting, where snowflakes were produced to decorate winter windows.

(1) Trace the template on page 125 onto card and cut it out. Cut a piece of baking parchment 18cm (7in) square and fold it in half. Fold it in half again, folding in the same direction. Crease the paper quite firmly each time.

(2) Position the template in the middle of the folded parchment and draw around it in pencil.

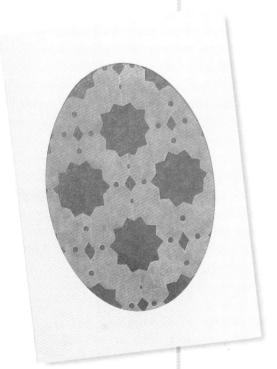

(3) Position the template just above the first outline, with half of it overlapping the folded edge of the parchment. Draw around it as before. Re-position it on the other side of the paper and draw around it again.

(4) Continue in this pattern of whole and half outlines. Work up to one end of the paper, then work down from the middle to the other end. Draw a free-hand diamond between each central outline, and half-diamonds between each half outline. The final pattern should look like this.

(5) Use the tips of sharp, pointed scissors to cut a slit in the middle of each shape, then cut out to the edges and around the outline. Ensure that you keep the folds in the paper on top of one another.

(6) Use a leather punch to punch small holes between the cut-outs.

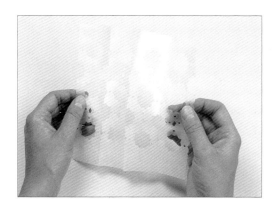

(7) Carefully unfold the parchment to reveal the lacy pattern. Lay a piece of scrap paper over the parchment and firmly rub over it to flatten creases in the parchment as much as possible.

(8) The lacy paper will make two cards, so cut it in half, then cut each piece slightly smaller than the central panel of an aperture card. Stick double-sided tape (see *Double-sided tape*, page 13) around the edges of the central panel. Peel off the backing and lay the lacy paper over the tape, centring it so that some tape is still exposed.

(9) Cut a piece of coloured paper slightly smaller than the lacy paper. Lay the coloured paper over the lacy paper, pressing it down onto the tape showing through the lace cut-outs and ensuring that it fills the whole aperture. Fold the card closed, pressing the covering panel down onto the remainder of the exposed tape.

leaf rubbings

Nature provides both inspiration and an abundance of material for the card maker, much of it being cost-free. A small flower press will allow you to collect and preserve suitable leaves and flowers. Do respect the countryside and never take rare flowers or damage plants and trees.

FRESH
LEAVES

You can use this technique with fresh leaves, but do test it on different types. If the leaves have a lot of sap in them, the sap can seep out and spoil the rubbing.

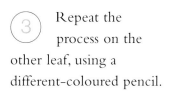

① Lay two pressed leaves face-down on scrap paper, so that the more prominent veins on the underside are facing up. Lay a piece of vellum, or thin paper, over them.

② Using a coloured pencil, rub gently over a leaf. Try not to colour outside the edges of the leaf.

③ Repeat the process on the other leaf, using a different-coloured pencil.

④ Spray glue (see *Adhesives*, page 16) onto the back of the piece of vellum and stick it onto a card.

microwaved flowers

The microwave oven offers a speedy way of drying and pressing flowers. For the best results, choose simple, fairly flat blooms, although composite flowers, such as hydrangea and verbena, can give good results if the flower heads are treated individually.

1 Lay kitchen paper on a flat, microwave-safe plate. Place a piece of blotting paper from a flower press on the kitchen paper.

2 Arrange flowers on the blotting paper. If they are not naturally flat, it is better to place them face down. Make sure that none of the flowers are touching each other. Lay another piece of blotting paper over the flowers.

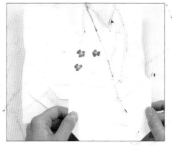

3 Lay kitchen paper over the blotting paper and put a flat-bottomed dish on top. Stand a dish of water on the flat-bottomed dish and put the whole stack into the microwave. Cook at full power for about two minutes (see right).

4 Take the stack out of the microwave and leave it to go cold. Once it is completely cold, remove the dishes and the top sheet of kitchen paper. Carefully lift off the top sheet of blotting paper to expose the pressed flowers.

5 Put a dot of all-purpose gel adhesive (see *Adhesives*, page 16) on the back of each flower in turn. Gently press the flowers onto the card. Leave the glue to dry.

MICROWAVE
TIMINGS

The time you need to 'cook' the flowers for will vary from type to type. It is best to experiment with a few flowers of a particular type and get the timing right before drying a lot.

string

String may not initially come to mind as a material for card decoration, but it is often to hand and can be used to create a pleasing design. Available in a range of types, weights and thicknesses, here, the natural texture and characteristics of garden twine have been exploited.

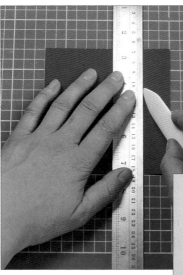

1 Using a bone folder, score a line approximately 2.5cm (1in) in from the folded edge of the card (see *Folding a card*, page 12). Do not press too hard, as you want to score the front of the card only.

2 Fold the front of the card open along the scored line.

3 Punch four evenly spaced holes through both layers of the card. Punch the holes just to the left of the score line, so that they are between the score line and the folded edge.

COLOURED
STRING

*String is sometimes
available in different
colours, so keep an eye
out for good colours and
buy them when you see
them. You can use the
same string to tie an
accompanying gift; fray
the ends as here.*

④   Cut a piece of string approximately 30cm (12in) long. Fold it in half and push the loop through the top hole, from the front of the card to the back.

⑤   Pass the ends of the string through the loop and pull it tight. Make sure that the loop and the ends are on the front of the card, tight up against the hole.

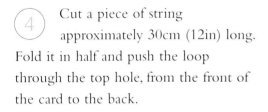

⑥   Tie the ends of the string in a double knot. Repeat the process for the remaining holes.

⑦   Trim the ends of the pieces of string to different lengths. Un-twist each end to fray it.

pieces from the scrapbag

Fabrics can inspire some splendid cards and most homes have some scraps tucked away. Keep off-cuts from other projects and old clothes, look out for remnants in stores and buy the odd patchwork fat-quarter; you will soon have the ingredients needed for a whole range of projects.

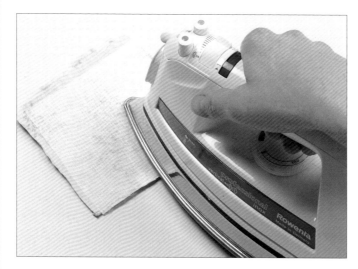

1 If you are using a fabric that will fray, iron a piece of fusible interfacing onto the back of it before you start the project.

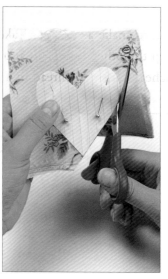

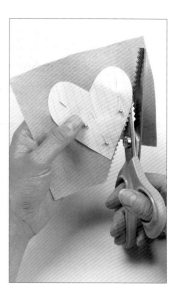

2 Photocopy the templates on page 125 and cut them out. Pin the smaller template onto patterned fabric and cut out the heart shape.

3 Pin the larger template to a piece of felt and cut around the heart shape with pinking shears.

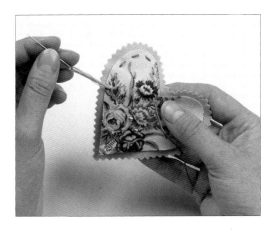

④ Pin the smaller heart to the centre of the larger one. Thread a needle with embroidery thread and start to stitch the two hearts together, working round from the top point. Leave a long tail of thread on the front of the hearts and stitch around one side with small running stitches.

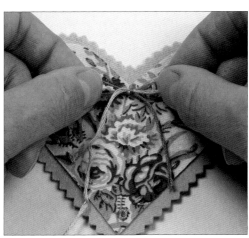

RECYCLING FABRICS

Making a card can be a great way to recycle pretty but often redundant items such as lace handkerchiefs or embroidered napkins. Recycling cloth from special garments or favourite items can add a nostalgic dimension to an anniversary or birthday card.

⑤ At the point of the hearts make a French knot. Stitch up the other side using small running stitches.

⑥ Take the needle off the thread. and tie the two ends of the thread in a bow. Trim the tails.

⑦ Using a leather punch, punch a pattern of tiny holes in the zig-zag edge of the felt.

⑧ Spread fabric glue over the back of the felt, inside the line of stitching (see *Adhesives*, page 16). Stick the heart to the front of a card.

THIS SECTION CONTAINS A DOZEN PROJECTS IN WHICH BASIC TECHNIQUES HAVE BEEN COMBINED TO MAKE A VARIETY OF CARDS SUITABLE FOR DIFFERENT OCCASIONS. WITH SOME INVENTIVE USE OF FAMILIAR ITEMS, THE CARDS HAVE BEEN DESIGNED TO MAKE THE BEST USE OF EVERYDAY MATERIALS. ONCE YOU HAVE GATHERED TOGETHER THE REQUIRED ELEMENTS, EACH CARD IS VERY STRAIGHTFORWARD TO MAKE.

pressed flowers

Pressed flowers presented in this way have a fresh and contemporary look that is far more appealing than traditional, rather tired arrangements. Ring the changes by experimenting with different types of labels.

materials

cosmetic sponge

pink ink pad

three circular paper tags

three microwaved pressed flowers

spray adhesive

three self-adhesive pads

12.5cm (5in) square white smooth card blank

leather punch

scissors

techniques

microwave flowers, *page 45*

punching shapes, *page 20*

self-adhesive pads, *page 18*

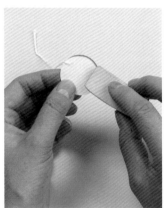

1 Dab the cosmetic sponge onto the stamp pad to pick up some ink.

2 Wipe a little colour around the edge of a tag. Repeat the process with the other two tags. Leave to dry.

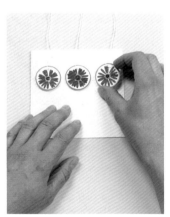

3 Lay the flowers face down and gently spray the backs with adhesive. Stick a flower to the centre of each tag.

4 Stick a self-adhesive pad to the back of each tag. Stick the tags in a row across the front of the card.

5 Using a leather punch, punch three holes near the top edge of the card. Align one hole directly above the centre of each tag.

6 Thread one of the strings of each tag through its aligned hole. Gently pull the string taut and tie it in a double knot on top of the card. Trim the ends short.

valentine's day

materials

paper lace doily

pencil

craft knife

cutting mat

low-tack spray
adhesive

11.5 x 18cm
(4½ x 7in) piece
of cream vellum

scrap paper

metallic pink stencil
spray paint

sharp scissors

decorative-edge
scissors

11.5 x 9cm
(4¼ x 3½ in)
cream card blank

embroidery needle

pink embroidery
thread

tiny microwaved
pressed flower

all-purpose
gel adhesive

techniques

spraying,
page 24

microwave flowers,
page 45

adhesives,
page 16

This pretty lace-effect card uses simple techniques to create a romantic greeting. If the Valentine is to be hand-delivered, a special touch is to wrap the card in a ribbon-tied doily instead of putting it in a conventional envelope.

 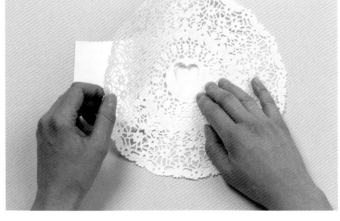

1 Draw a heart on the centre panel of the doily. Using the craft knife on the cutting mat, cut out the heart.

2 Spray some low-tack adhesive onto the back of the doily and stick it to the vellum. Position the doily on the vellum towards the right-hand side, so that the heart is centred on what will be the front of the card.

3 Lay both the doily and vellum on scrap paper and spray over them with the pink paint.

4 Carefully peel the doily off the vellum to reveal the lace and heart pattern. Leave to dry.

5 Draw a smaller heart inside the sprayed one and cut it out with the sharp scissors.

6 Cut the edges of the vellum with the decorative scissors. Fold the vellum in half.

7 Lay the vellum over the card, aligning the spine folds. Thread the needle with a length of embroidery thread. Push the needle through the spine, 1cm (½ in) above the centre point, and bring it back through 2cm (1in) lower down. Tie the ends in a knot and trim them short.

8 Using the all-purpose gel adhesive, stick the microwaved pressed flower through the centre of the cut-out heart onto the front of the card.

pop-up flowers

materials

12cm (4¾ in) square
pale green smooth
card blank

scallop-edged scissors

12 x 10cm
(4¾ x 4in)
piece of pink
gingham paper

scrap paper

spray adhesive

brayer

two 10 x 2cm
(4 x ¾ in) strips
of pale green,
smooth, thin card

steel rule

cutting mat

bone folder

double-sided tape

two stickers of
flowers in pots

sheet of acetate

sharp scissors

techniques

double-sided tape,
page 13

simple pop-up card,
page 33

folding a card,
page 12

A variation on the simple pop-up card, this design is made with separate tabs stuck inside the card, which have the added advantage of not affecting the front of the card. So do stick an additional motif on the front to decorate that, too.

1 Trim the leading edge of the front of the card with the scallop-edged scissors.

2 Trim one long edge of the pink gingham paper with the scallop-edged scissors.

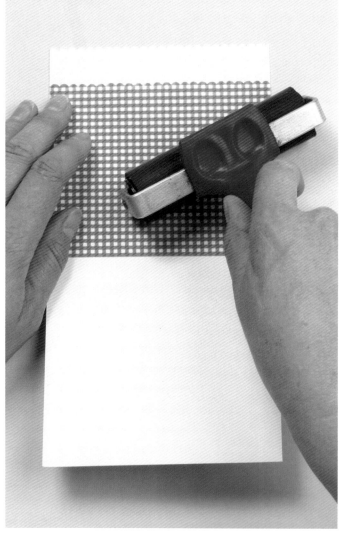

3 Lay the gingham paper face-down on the scrap paper and spray the back with adhesive. Stick the gingham to the inside-front of the card, aligning the straight edge with the fold in the card. Roll over the gingham paper with a brayer to ensure that it is firmly stuck down.

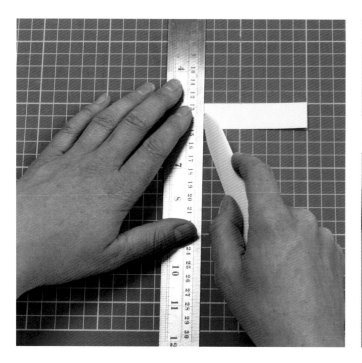

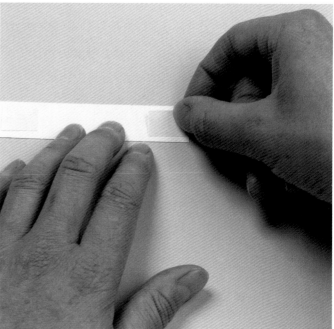

4 To make the tabs, use the bone folder to score a line across both strips of card at every 2.5cm (1in). Trim 1mm (1/16 in) off each end of both strips.

5 Stick a piece of double-sided tape to each end of both strips, within the scored sections.

6 Fold each strip in half along the central scored line. Peel the backing off the tape on one end.

7 Stick one end of one strip to the gingham paper, positioning it 3cm (1 1/4 in) in from the edge of the card and 1mm (1/16 in) from the fold. Stick the other strip 3cm (1 1/4 in) in from the other side of the card.

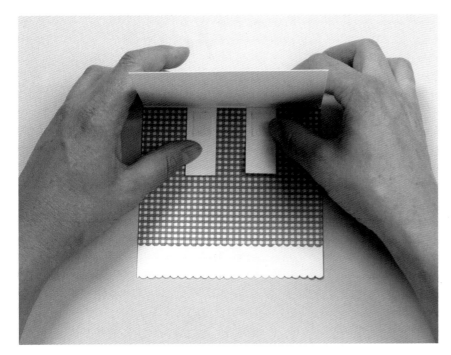

8 Peel the backing off the tape on the other ends of the strips. Keeping the strips folded, close the card on top of them. Press firmly to ensure that the strips are well stuck to the front and back of the card. Open out the card again and the strips should bend on the other two scored lines to form an open box shape.

9 Stick the stickers onto the sheet of acetate.

10 Using the sharp scissors, carefully cut the stickers out.

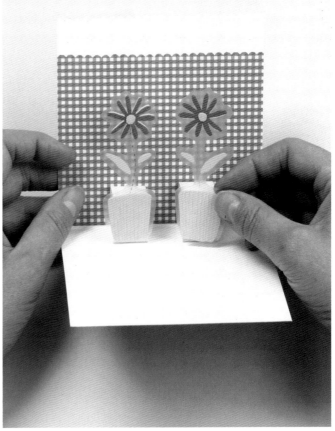

11 Stick a piece of double-sided tape to the back of each flowerpot. Peel off the backing and stick the pots to the card tabs.

colourful christmas

A modern interpretation of a favourite festive motif, this card can be worked in colours to suit your own Christmas theme. You could also try using the same techniques with other simple seasonal shapes, such as stars or snowflakes.

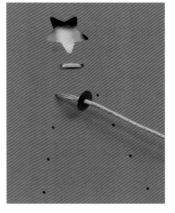

1 Trace off the template onto the piece of tracing paper. Lay the paper over the front of the card and punch out the star.

2 Using the pin, pierce holes through the card at the points marked on the template.

3 Thread the needle with a long length of embroidery thread and tie a knot in one end. Push the needle through the top left-hand hole, from back to front, and pull the thread through right up to the knot.

4 Take the needle down through the top right-hand hole to make the first stitch. Bring it back up through the next left-hand hole, thread on a sequin, then push the needle down through the parallel right-hand hole.

5 Continue, threading sequins onto each stitch, until the tree is complete. Fasten off the thread on the back. With the card closed, glue the star sequin through the star aperture to the inside back of the card.

shooting stars

This dramatic card could be used for sending Christmas greetings or as an invite to a fireworks party. Invent similar cards for other occasions by changing the motif and colourway; heart-shaped sequins on a pink background for a Valentine, perhaps.

1 Score the card 8.5cm (3¾ in) from one short end. Machine curving lines from the score line across the short, front section of the card, using the main picture as a guide.

2 Fold the threads on the leading edge to the back and lay lengths of craft wire over them. Using black tape, tape the wire in place: on the front the wire should continue the lines of stitching.

3 Trim the wires so they are different lengths, both shorter than the back of the card. Put a dot of all-purpose adhesive on the back of a large star sequin and lay the end of a wire on it. Lay another sequin on top. Repeat the process with the end of the other wire.

4 Using the glue pen, put some tiny dots of adhesive on the front and the inside back of the card, positioning them around the lines of stitching and wires. Dampen the end of the cocktail stick, pick up tiny star sequins and put them on the dots of adhesive.

birthday girl

materials

sheet of gift wrap

scissors

pale green
opalescent paper

spray glue

brayer

scallop-edge scissors

10 x 15cm (4 x 6in)
pink and red duplex
card blank

thin card

small self-adhesive
pads

silver narrow ribbon

two flower beads

techniques

adhesives,
page 16

self-adhesive pads,
page 18

gift wrap,
page 39

This way of using gift wrap incorporates relief to add extra interest. Individual motifs are used, so you will need wrap that has a repeat pattern. The size of the card will depend on the scale of the pattern. For a co-ordinated look, package a gift in the remaining wrap.

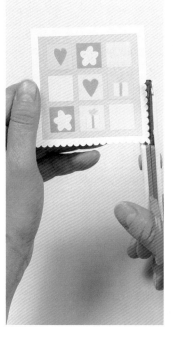

1 Roughly cut out the two identical sections of the gift wrap that you want to use.

2 Trim one of the sections to size. Cut the opalescent paper 0.5cm (¼ in) larger than the section. Spray glue onto the back of the gift wrap and stick it to the paper. Roll over the wrap with the brayer to ensure that it is firmly stuck. Cut a decorative edge around the paper with the scallop-edge scissors.

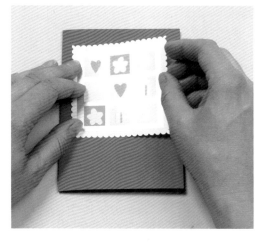

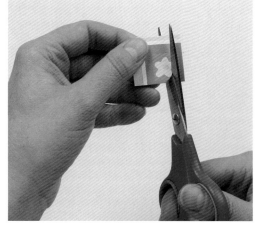

3 Spray glue over the back of the panel and stick it to the front of the card, positioning it towards the top.

4 Spray glue over the back of the remaining piece of gift wrap and stick it to the thin card. Cut individual motifs out of the gift wrap.

5 Stick a self-adhesive pad to the back of each motif. Stick the motif exactly over the corresponding motif on the panel.

6 Tie a length of ribbon around the fold in the card. Tie a flower bead to each end of the ribbon.

big number

materials

15 x 10cm (6 x 4in)
green and yellow
duplex card blank

pencil

steel rule

craft knife

cutting mat

soft eraser

coloured stickers

techniques

folding a card,
page 12

punching shapes,
page 20

simple shaped card,
page 32

Bold and graphic, this technique can be adapted to incorporate single or double numbers, though is perhaps best avoided if the recipient is a little age-sensitive! In another context, the number could relate to a special anniversary or even a new house.

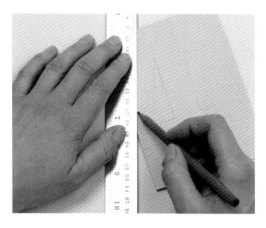
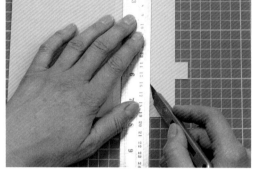

1 Draw the number you want onto the front of the card. Some part of it must butt against the fold in the card.

2 Lay the card out flat and, using the craft knife on the cutting mat, cut out the number. Use the steel rule to cut along straight lines.

3 Remember that some part of the number needs to remain attached to the back of the card. So cut carefully along the spine to the section that is going to stay attached. Rub out any pencil marks.

4 Decorate the number with the stickers or with shapes punched out of coloured paper.

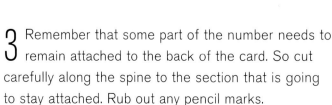

happy anniversary

materials

This pretty card could easily be adapted to suit the beads and sequins you have, and the occasion it is celebrating. A Christmas version could use silver beads and a snowflake sequin, for example. Include some loose sequins in the envelope as a surprise element.

materials

purple and mauve duplex card

pencil

steel rule

craft knife

cutting mat

sharp needle

multi-coloured machine embroidery thread

sixteen tiny beads in shades of purple

five tiny opalescent heart sequins

one opalescent outline heart sequin

glue pen

techniques

folding a card, *page 12*

adhesives, *page 16*

hand stitching, *page 36*

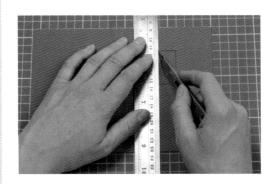

1 Cut and score the card to make a 15 x 10cm (6 x 4in) card blank. Using the pencil and rule, measure and mark out a 2 x 4cm (³⁄₄ in x 1¹⁄₂ in) aperture on the centre front. Using the craft knife and steel rule on the cutting mat, carefully cut out the aperture.

2 Thread the needle, thread on a bead, then put the free end of the thread through the needle, so the bead is on a loop. Align the ends of the thread. From front to back, push the needle through the card just above the centre top of the aperture.

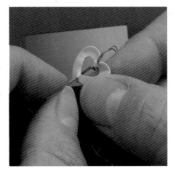

3 Pull the thread through up to the bead. Thread four beads, a heart sequin and another bead onto the needle and push them up to the top of the aperture.

4 Push the needle through the top of the outline heart sequin. Thread on a bead and then push the needle through the bottom of the sequin.

5 Thread on eight more beads. From back to front, push the needle through the card just below the centre bottom of the aperture. Pull the thread taut.

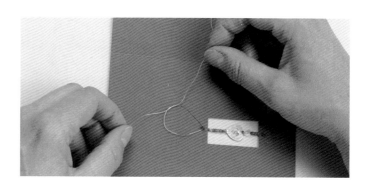

6 Thread another bead onto the needle, then push the needle back through the hole it came out of.

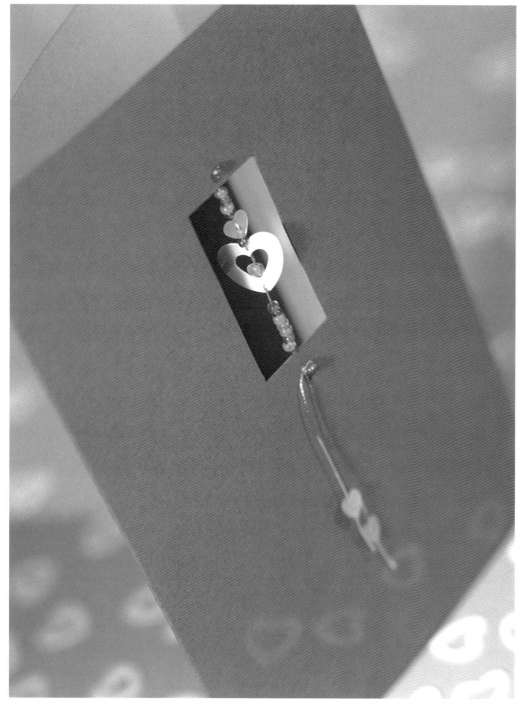

7 Pass the needle twice around the thread on the back of the card, then bring it back out to the front through the same hole. Take the needle off the thread and tie the ends of the thread in a double knot.

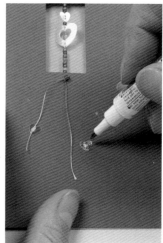

8 Lay one of the heart sequins on the card and use the glue pen to put a dot of adhesive on it. Lay one of the threads on the adhesive, then lay another sequin on top. Repeat the process with the other thread.

punched flowers

materials

craft knife

steel rule

cutting mat

10 x 15cm (4 x 6in)
cream, ridged
card blank

circular aperture
hobby punch

narrow double-
sided tape

10 x 15cm (4 x 6in)
pale green vellum
internal leaf

flower hobby punch

scraps of cream
and green
opalescent paper

paper adhesive

silver three-
dimensional paint

cream narrow ribbon

scissors

techniques

adhesives,
page 16

punching shapes,
page 20

punching apertures,
page 22

internal leaf,
page 88

This card is so quick to produce; in fact the concept is one that can be revisited time after time, using the positive and negative pieces of punched paper in different ways. For a change, try cutting the leading edge of the card with decorative scissors.

1 Using the craft knife and steel rule on the cutting mat, trim 0.5cm (¼ in) off the leading edge of the front of the card.

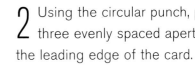

2 Using the circular punch, punch three evenly spaced apertures down the leading edge of the card.

3 Open the card out and stick a length of double-sided tape down the inside front edge, close to the fold. Peel off the backing paper.

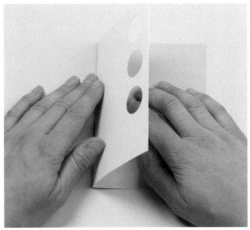

4 Lay the folded internal leaf on the inside back of the card, aligning the edges with the edges of the card. Close the card onto it so that the tape sticks to the front of the leaf.

5 Using the flower punch, punch one cream flower and two green flowers out of the opalescent paper. Apply paper adhesive to the back of each punched-out flower. Stick the flowers to the internal leaf, positioning one in the middle of each aperture.

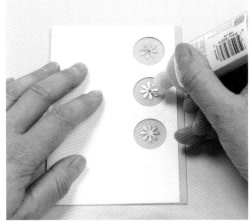

6 Add a dot of three-dimensional paint to the centre of each flower.

7 Tie a length of narrow ribbon around the fold in the card and trim the ends at a slant.

buttoned up

A buttonband from a worn-out shirt is the basis of this card. Classic shirts have several buttons and buttonholes that can be used, and two shirts will provide enough contrasting fabrics to make lots of cards. If you prefer you can glue or hand-stitch the square to the card.

materials

iron

piece of iron-on interfacing

piece of gingham fabric

scissors

button

sewing threads

needle

button-band of a gingham shirt

sewing machine

12cm (4¾in) square white smooth card blank

techniques

machine stitching, *page 23*

pieces from the scrapbag, *page 48*

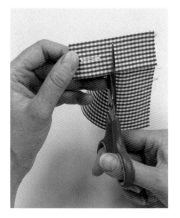

1 Iron the interfacing onto the back of the gingham fabric. Cut out a square of gingham, cutting along the lines of the pattern.

2 Using a contrast-colour thread, stitch a button to the centre of the gingham square.

3 Cut out a square from the button band, with a button hole in the centre of the square. Again, cut along the lines of the gingham pattern.

4 Button the square of shirt onto the button.

5 Using a toning-colour thread, machine stitch the square of gingham to the front of the card. Stitch along a line of the pattern. You can glue the square to the card first to hold it in position while you stitch.

flowerpot

materials

15 x 10cm (6 x 4in)
purple and orange
duplex card blank

pencil

steel rule

craft knife

cutting mat

scrap of opalescent
purple and plain red
thin card

leather punch

flower hobby punch

lime green
embroidery thread

self-adhesive pads

silver craft wire

double-sided tape

sticky tape

silver three-
dimensional paint

purple pen

This cheerful card uses unusual presentation techniques and layout to highlight the design, which is further emphasized by relief effects. The miniature message card could carry good luck or get well wishes, making this a useful, multi-purpose greeting card.

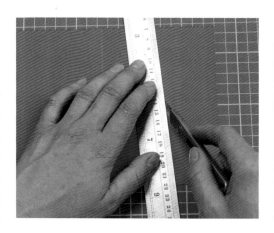

1 Open the card out flat and draw a diagonal line across it. At the top the line is 5cm (2in) from the fold, and at the bottom 6.5cm (2½ in) from the fold. Using the craft knife and steel rule on the cutting mat, cut along the line.

2 Trace off the flowerpot template on page 126 and transfer it onto the opalescent card. Using the steel rule and craft knife on the cutting mat, cut out the shape.

techniques

double-sided tape,
page 13

self-adhesive pads,
page 18

punching shapes,
page 20

wire,
page 41

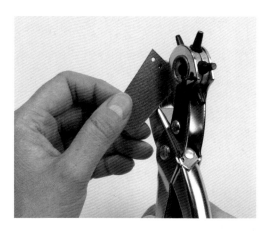

3 Using the leather punch, punch a row of tiny decorative holes across the top of the pot.

4 Using the flower punch, punch one flower each out of the opalescent and red cards and one out of the purple side of the card cut from the front.

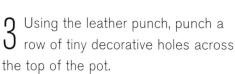

5 Lay the end of a length of embroidery thread on the back of a flower and stick a self-adhesive pad over it. Repeat the process with the other two flowers.

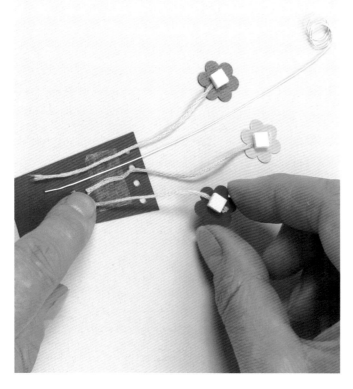

6 Wind one end of a length of craft wire three times around a pencil. Slide the wire off the pencil and flatten the coil.

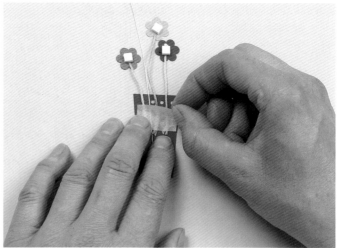

7 Stick a piece of double-sided tape to the back of the flowerpot and peel off the backing. Stick the free ends of the embroidery threads to it, arranging them so that the flowers are at different heights. Stick the straight end of the wire to the tape, too.

8 Stick a piece of sticky tape over all the ends to secure them. Stick a self-adhesive pad to the top and bottom of the pot.

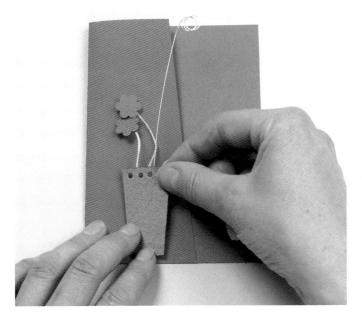

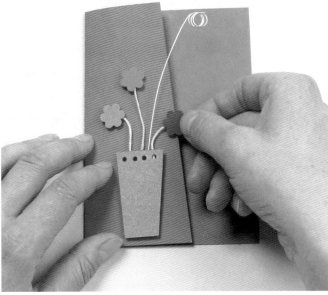

9 Peel the backing off the pads on the flowerpot and stick it to the front of the card. The bottom of the pot should be just above the bottom of the card.

10 Peel the backing off the pads on the backs of the flowers and stick them to the front of the card, ensuring that they are at different heights.

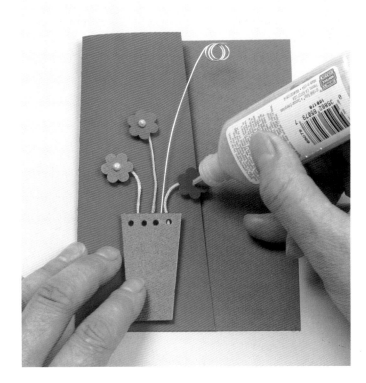

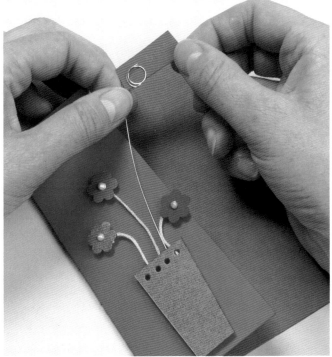

11 Put a dot of three-dimensional paint in the centre of each flower.

12 Write the recipient's name on the orange side of a scrap of the card that was cut off the front and tuck it into the wire coils.

birthday boy

materials

15cm (6in) square of holographic paper

selection of washers of different sizes

matt black enamel spray paint

10cm (4in) square of cream, smooth thin card

pencil

steel rule

craft knife

cutting mat

double-sided tape

12cm (4¾ in) square cream textured card blank

four tiny black paper fasteners

techniques

double-sided tape, *page 13*

paper fasteners, *page 19*

spraying, *page 24*

An eye-catching card aimed to please to the younger men in our lives, particularly those who are into CDs and music. This card involves using spray paint and some everyday hardware, with ingenious results. Cool!

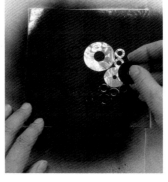

1 Lay the holographic paper on scrap paper. Arrange the washers on the holographic paper, butting them up to make a dense pattern.

2 Spray over the paper and washers until the paper is completely black. Leave to dry. Lift the washers off to reveal holographic rings.

3 Draw a 1.5cm- (½ in-) wide frame on the smooth cream card. Using the steel rule and craft knife, cut out the frame.

4 Lay the frame in position on the sprayed paper and draw around it. Using the steel rule and craft knife, cut out the square of paper, cutting 0.5cm (¼ in) inside the drawn line.

5 Stick lengths of double-sided tape to the back of the frame. Peel off the backings and stick the frame to the paper, centring it so that some of the tape is still exposed.

6 Stick the sprayed
  panel to the front of
the card.

7 Lay the card out flat
  and, using the craft
knife, cut a tiny slot in
each corner of the frame,
cutting through the frame
and the front of the card.
Put a paper fastener
through each slot and
open out the legs at
the back.

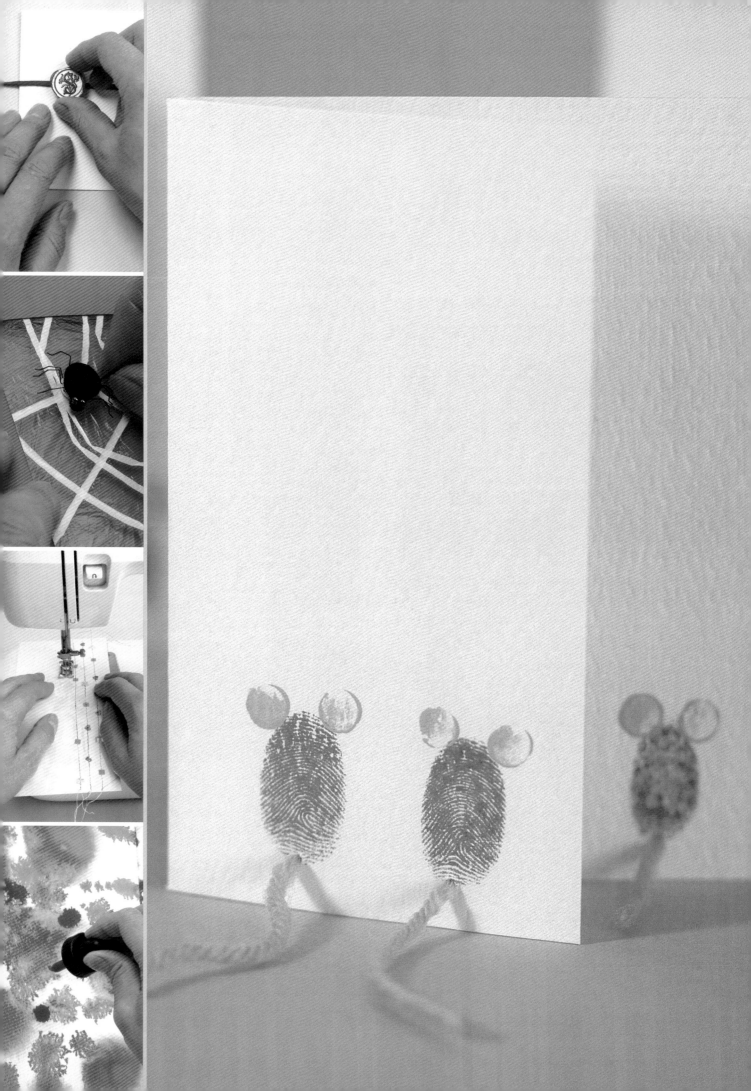

batch cards

There are many occasions on which multiple cards are needed – Christmas cards, birth announcements or wedding invitations, for example. Creating your own cards in quantities can seem daunting, but this chapter is full of good ideas for making the process as speedy as possible, while keeping the cards stylish. The techniques section has simple ideas that can be used alone to make a card. The project section combines techniques to produce creative cards for all occasions. Some cards, such as Christmas cards, where you are likely to be making a good many, are very quick and simple. Other designs, like party invitations, where you will need fewer, can be a little more involved.

THIS SECTION
ILLUSTRATES A NUMBER
OF TECHNIQUES THAT CAN
HELP YOU OVERCOME
VARIOUS PROBLEMS
ASSOCIATED WITH MAKING
BATCHES OF CARDS.
SOME TECHNIQUES DEAL
WITH USING IMAGES,
OTHERS WITH
INCORPORATING TEXT,
AND THERE ARE ALSO
IDEAS FOR DECORATING
LARGE SURFACES THAT
CAN BE USED AS THE
BASIS FOR MAKING A
NUMBER OF CARDS AT
THE SAME TIME.

sepia tinting

Special celebrations, such as a ruby wedding, demand a special invitation and old photographs or documents make ideal material. Black and white photocopies are an inexpensive solution but lack the character of the original. Tone down the stark appearance with a simple tinting process.

1 Photocopy the picture onto thin card. Mix up a strong solution of instant coffee granules and a little water, stirring it well to make sure that all the granules have dissolved. Dip a cotton wool ball into the solution and wipe it over the photocopy, tinting it a sepia colour.

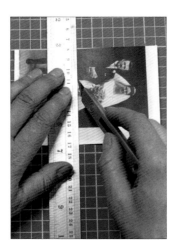

2 When the photocopy is dry, cut it out with a craft knife and steel rule on a cutting mat.

3 Slip a black photo corner onto each corner of the copy.

4 Dampen the back of the photo corners and stick the whole panel on to a card.

transferring an image

Cellulose thinners can be used to transfer a black-and-white photocopy or computer-generated image directly onto a card. The outcome will be affected by the paper, image density, time taken, the tool used and pressure applied. A photocopy can often be used more than once.

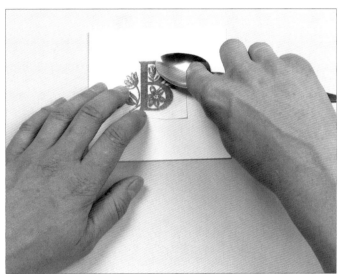

1. Dip the tip of a cotton bud into cellulose thinners and wipe it over the back of a photocopied image. The whole image must be dampened, but must not be soaked.

2. Lay the photocopy face-down in position on the card. Rub firmly over the back of the image with the bowl of a metal spoon. The thinners make the paper translucent so it is easy to see the image and ensure that you rub over all of it. Hold the photocopy firmly in place while you are rubbing so that it does not move and smudge the image.

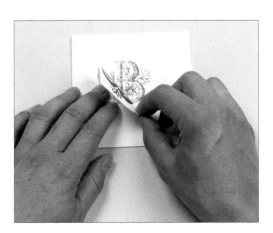

3. Carefully peel off the photocopy to reveal the transferred image. Leave to dry.

colour print

Many of us have access to a computer and colour printer, ideal tools for producing multiple coloured images inexpensively. With a digital camera or scanner you can use your own images to create lovely, personal cards. Otherwise, take the image to a copy shop and have them reproduce it.

①   Print out the picture, getting as many prints as possible on each sheet of paper. Cut out the prints and trim them down so that they fit in the aperture card you want to use.

②   Stick lengths of narrow double-sided tape around the edges of the back of the aperture.

③   Peel the backing off the tape. Lay the picture face-up on a flat surface. Hold the aperture over it and position it so that the picture is framed as you want it to be. Lay the card on the picture. Press it down to ensure that it is well stuck.

④   Stick lengths of tape around the edges of the panel that will cover the aperture.

⑤   Peel the backing off the tape. Fold the panel over the aperture and press down.

rubber stamp

A stamp enables you to reproduce a motif many times and though there are various methods of making a stamp this is one of the quickest. Try adding embellishments to the stamped design with three-dimensional paint, sequins, gems, accent beads or perhaps the punch itself.

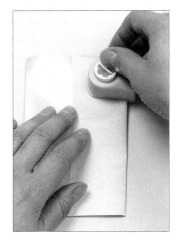

SELF-ADHESIVE RUBBER

(1) Using a hobby punch, punch shapes out of a sheet of self-adhesive rubber.

(2) Peel the backing off each of the punched shapes.

(3) Stick the punched shapes onto a plastic lid; the lid of a food container is ideal.

It can be difficult to slide the rubber into the punch, so fold a piece of greaseproof paper over it first. The smooth surface of the greaseproof allows you to slide the rubber easily into the punch.

(4) Press the stamp gently down onto an ink pad, ensuring that the rubber shapes are evenly coated with ink.

(5) Press the stamp down firmly onto a card. Lift the stamp off cleanly to reveal the design. Add any embellishments you want to use.

string stamp

Names or words can be difficult to make into a rubber stamp, so turn to strong, flexible, universally available string. Choose medium-weight, smooth string for the best results. The same technique can be used to make figurative or abstract designs, too.

LETTERS

A flowing style of handwriting is the easiest and most effective type to use with a string stamp, as you can curve the string to fit the letters more easily.

① Write the name you want to stamp on a piece of tracing paper the same size as the front of the card. Position the name where you want it to appear on the card. Scribble over the name with a soft pencil, scribbling on the front.

② Lay the tracing paper scribble-side down on a piece of thick card. Draw over the name so that it is transferred in reverse onto the front of the card.

③ Squeeze a trail of craft or fabric adhesive over the traced name, following the lines as accurately as possible.

DECORATING

(4) Stick string over the glued lines. Work with a long length of string, pressing it down onto the glue and cutting it off at appropriate points. Cut the string at an angle so that the cut ends will sit neatly against one another. When it is complete, lay the stamp face-down on a piece of greaseproof paper and lay a heavy book on top of it. Leave to dry.

(5) Cut the card stamp backing to the same size as the tracing paper, so that the stamp is the same size as the card front. Dab an ink pad onto the string to ink it up.

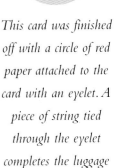

This card was finished off with a circle of red paper attached to the card with an eyelet. A piece of string tied through the eyelet completes the luggage tag effect.

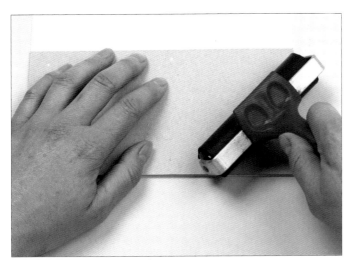

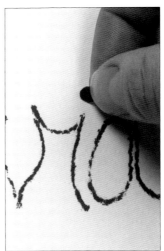

(6) Open the card out flat and press the stamp down on the front of it, aligning the bottom and sides of the stamp with three edges of the card. Roll over the back of the stamp with a brayer to ensure that all of the inked string comes into contact with the card.

(7) If the name has an 'i' or 'j' in it, punch a small circle of contrast colour paper and use this to dot the letter.

embossed wallpaper

This is a great way to give cards the elegant, embossed effect associated with complex or time-consuming processes. It looks most convincing when the wallpaper matches the colour and texture of the card. A good, inexpensive technique for wedding invitations and formal stationery.

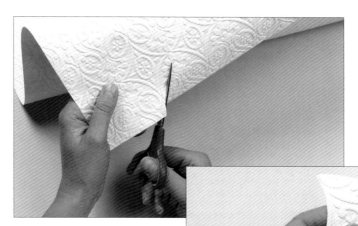

You need to look at wallpaper in a different way for this technique. The overall pattern isn't important, it's the details you are interested in.

(1) Select the section of the wallpaper you would like to use and cut it out roughly.

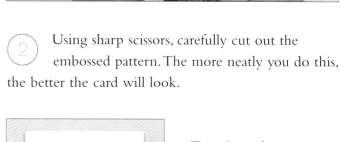

(2) Using sharp scissors, carefully cut out the embossed pattern. The more neatly you do this, the better the card will look.

(3) Spread paper adhesive on the back of the cut-out section, making sure that you apply the adhesive right up to the edges. Stick the section to a matching-colour card.

faux seal

It can be quite tricky to make wax seals and the result is often less than perfect. This quick and uncomplicated method uses a modern material that is easy to work with and flexible, even when the seal is finished. As the seals are made separately and glued on, you never risk ruining a card.

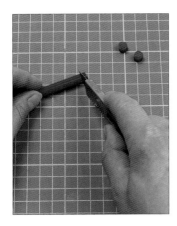

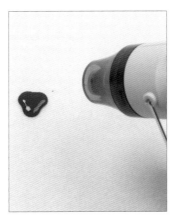

① Using a craft knife, cut three narrow slices off a coloured glue stick.

② Place the three slices together on a sheet of greaseproof paper. Use a heat gun to melt the slices until they start to fuse together.

③ Press a seal stamp onto a silver ink pad, then press it onto the soft glue. If the glue has hardened, you can re-soften it with the heat gun. Leave the stamp in place for a minute until the glue hardens a little.

MASS-PRODUCING SEALS

To make lots of seals, arrange as many groups of slices as you need on the greaseproof paper. Heat all the groups, then go back and soften and stamp each group in turn.

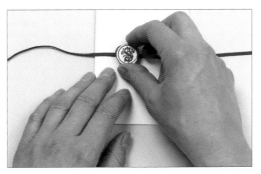

④ Lift the stamp off to reveal the coloured seal.

⑤ Lay a length of ribbon around the card. Put a dab of all-purpose adhesive on the back of the seal and stick it to the front of the card, over the ribbon. Leave to dry, then tie the ends of the ribbon in a bow.

internal leaf

An internal leaf is a practical way to incorporate text in invitations and many other cards. The words can be produced on a computer or photocopier before the leaf is made up. If the card has an aperture the internal leaf will be visible, giving the opportunity to play with colour.

INTERNAL LEAF

The leaf should be up to 0.5cm (¼in) smaller all around than the card. This allows it to sit neatly inside the card without the edges showing when the card is closed.

① Punch a shape in the front of a card. This is not essential, but it allows the colour of the leaf to show through, adding decoration to the front of the card.

② Slip the internal leaf into the card, centring it so that an equal border of card shows at each edge.

③ Tie a length of narrow ribbon around the fold of the card and leaf, fastening them together. Tie the ends in a neat bow and trim them.

attached panel

This is an elegant alternative to simply gluing a panel onto a card. Panels can be cut from large pieces of decorated paper, so this technique is well suited to batch cards. It is also ideal where text is needed, as the words can be printed out, the paper cut to size and then attached to the card.

1 Stick small pieces of double-sided tape to the back of the panel. Peel off the backing and stick the panel to the front of the card.

2 Mark two slots about 1cm (½in) apart. Using a craft knife and steel rule, cut the slots through the panel and the front of the card.

3 Thread an embroidery needle with a length of ribbon. Push the needle through the right-hand slot and bring it back out through the left-hand slot.

DIFFERENT RIBBONS

The thickness and width of the ribbon will dictate the length of the slots. Organza ribbon compresses easily so you can cut small slots and it will spread out to make full tails. Thicker ribbon will not compress so much and the slots will need to be wider. Work out the right size slot for your ribbon on scrap paper first.

4 Pull a length of ribbon through. Take the needle back down through the right-hand slot, above or below the ribbon already there.

5 Bring the needle back out through the left-hand slot, above or below the ribbon already there.

6 Arrange the ends and trim them both at the same angle.

bubble printing

A fun technique that makes an interesting background for decorations such as sequins, badges, photographs, collage or found objects. Here, stickers have been applied to a panel cut from a larger piece. This can be a good technique for children, though adult supervision is recommended.

1 Mix a solution of two parts water, one part ink and two parts washing-up detergent. Mix the solution in a jar and then tip it into a flat dish, wide enough to lay the card in.

2 Rest one end of the dish on a plate to tip it so that the ink solution is at one end of the dish. Put one end of a straw into the solution and blow through it to create bubbles.

BUBBLES

If the bubbles burst before enough colour has transferred onto the card, blow more and touch the paper onto them again. You can build up layers of pattern in this way, using different colours if you wish.

③ Lower one half of a piece of card onto the bubbles. Do not allow the card to touch the ink solution itself, just the bubbles. Turn the card around and lower the other half onto the bubbles. Leave the card to dry. Tip the ink solution back into the jar for future use.

④ Cut a strip of bubble card to the width of the card you want to decorate.

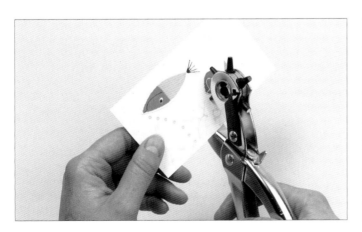

⑤ Decorate the strip with stickers: fish stickers work well on blue bubbles. Using a leather punch, punch some tiny holes to represent air bubbles.

⑥ Stick self-adhesive pads onto the back of the panel and stick it to a card.

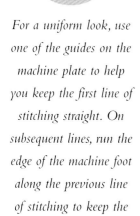

decorative stitching

Simple machine stitching is especially suitable for long strips of paper that can then be cut to size; in fact, this is better than attempting to start and stop neatly on pre-cut panels. Sequins, confetti or punched paper shapes are easy to sew over and could be chosen to reflect the occasion.

PARALLEL LINES

For a uniform look, use one of the guides on the machine plate to help you keep the first line of stitching straight. On subsequent lines, run the edge of the machine foot along the previous line of stitching to keep the lines parallel.

1 Cut a strip of paper. Using vari-coloured thread, machine straight lines across the paper. Periodically place a sequin on the paper and stitch over it. Cover the whole piece of paper with parallel lines of stitching.

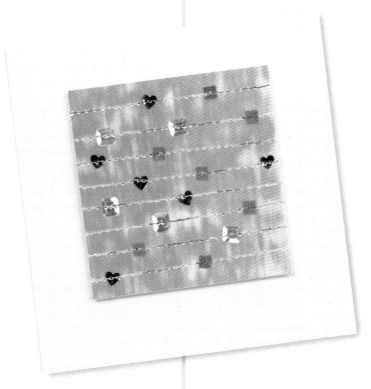

2 Using a craft knife and steel rule, cut the machined paper into squares or rectangles of the size you want.

3 Stick a self-adhesive pad to each corner of a square. Position the square centrally on the front of a card and stick it down.

dripping ink

This technique produces exciting effects that can provide a background for other applications but are decorative enough to stand alone. Pearlized inks can add further interest. Another great technique for children as it's quick and easy to decorate sheets of paper that are cut to size when dry.

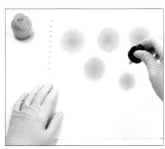

① Dip a foam brush into water and wipe it over the surface of some watercolour paper.

② Using the dropper in the lid of an ink bottle, drip spots of ink over the surface.

③ Dip a paintbrush into a different colour ink. Hold it over the paper and tap it just above the bristles to flick ink onto the paper.

WET PAPER

Do not soak the paper when you wet it. The degree of wetness will affect how far the ink spreads on the paper, and different types of ink will spread to different extents. The result will not be stable until the paper is completely dry.

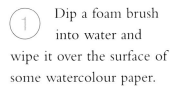

④ Flick more ink in a third colour onto the paper. Leave the paper to dry flat.

⑤ Cut a strip of inked paper and a strip of plain coloured paper. The strip of coloured paper should be wider than the inked paper. Using double-sided tape, stick the inked paper to the coloured paper, positioning it centrally.

⑥ Cut the assembled strip into sections the width of a card. Stick one section to the front of each card.

fusing polythene

Plastic bags can be recycled to make a 'stained-glass' material that looks effective mounted against a light background, as here. Alternatively, cut an aperture in the central and backing panel of an aperture card and mount the polythene between them so that light can shine through it.

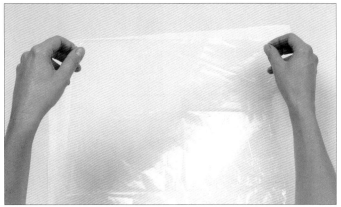

1 Cut a thin, clear polythene bag open and lay it flat over a sheet of greaseproof paper.

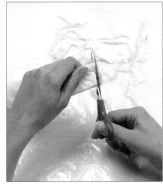

2 Roll up a selection of different-coloured plastic bags. Using scissors, cut slices off the roll to produce strands of coloured plastic.

3 Tear further strands off a another different-coloured plastic bag. Arrange all the strands on half of the sheet of polythene.

4 Fold the other half of the polythene over the strands.

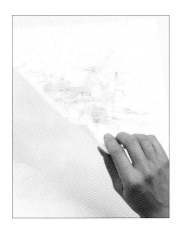

5 Lay another sheet of greaseproof paper over the top.

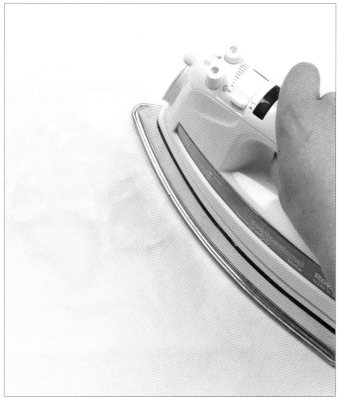

6 Set a domestic iron to a warm heat. Place the iron on one spot and hold it there for just a few seconds. Lift it off and reposition it on another spot. Repeat until you have fused the layers of polythene and plastic together.

POLYTHENE

Have fun incorporating text from the bags, or even small items such as sequins that can be fused into the polythene sandwich.

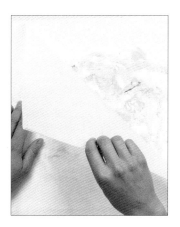

7 Remove the greaseproof paper to reveal the sheet of fused polythene.

8 Cut the sheet of fused polythene into squares large enough to fit behind the aperture of the card you are using.

9 Use lengths of double-sided tape to stick the square behind the aperture.

TEN PROJECTS ARE SHOWN
IN THIS SECTION,
COVERING A RANGE OF
DIFFERENT OCCASIONS.
ALL OF THEM HAVE BEEN
DESIGNED TO MAKE IT
PRACTICAL TO PRODUCE A
NUMBER OF SIMILAR
CARDS, THOUGH SOME ARE
BETTER SUITED FOR
SMALLER QUANTITIES.
HOPEFULLY THESE DESIGNS
WILL INSPIRE YOU TO TAKE
ON LARGER PROJECTS,
ADAPTING THEM TO YOUR
OWN NEEDS AND TASTES.

new baby

Personalised birth announcement cards can be reasonably quick to make. Purchase card blanks and apply your own stamped decoration, or leave them plain if time is short. You could mount a picture of the baby onto card and attach that to the front instead of a name.

materials

13cm (5in) square pink cards

scrap paper

baby shoes stamp

pearlized pink ink pad

sheets of cream thin card

computer

colour printer

craft knife

steel rule

cutting mat

cosmetic sponge

corner-rounding punch

invisible mounts

1.5cm- (¾ in-) wide pink satin ribbon

scissors

techniques

double-sided tape, *page 13*

stamping, *page 29*

attached panel, *page 89*

1 Open the cards out flat and lay them face-up on scrap paper. Stamp an all-over pattern of baby shoes, allowing some of the images to run over the edges of the card onto the scrap paper. Leave to dry.

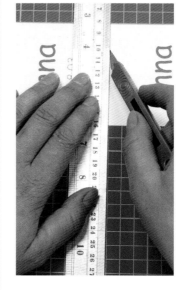

2 Print the name and date of birth in pink on the cream paper. The paper will be cut into squares, so fit as many names as possible onto a sheet. Using the craft knife and steel rule on the cutting mat, cut the sheets of paper into 8cm (3in) squares, with a name centred on each.

3 Dab the cosmetic sponge onto the ink pad to pick up colour. Wipe the sponge along the edges of each square to make a coloured border. Leave to dry.

4 Use the corner-rounding punch to round off the corners of each card and each square of cream paper.

5 Stick an invisible mount to the two upper corners of a cream square. Stick the cream square to the centre of a card front.

anna

6.8.03

6 Using the craft knife, cut two slots through the cream square and the card front. The slots should be approximately 1cm (½ in) from the top of the cream square, 1.5cm (¾ in) apart and 0.75cm (¼ in) long.

7 Tie the ribbon through the slots. Trim the ends to the same angle.

40th birthday party

This card is quick to make and lends itself well to production in larger quantities. It is ideal where text is needed as this can be printed on the leaf with the number. Different punches and colours could be used for teenage or children's parties, or a change of address card.

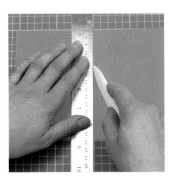

1 Using the steel rule and craft knife on the cutting mat, cut the card into 21 x 15cm (8¼ x 6in) rectangles. Mark the halfway point and score a line (this card was scored on the inside).

2 Slide the punch over the front edge of each card, aligning the top edge of the punch with the top of the card. Punch an aperture in each card.

3 Punch a row of slots in the leading and bottom edges of the card front.

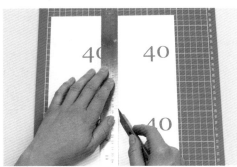

4 Print out the number 40 and the details of the party on the white card in plum ink. Cut the paper into 12 x 9cm (4½ x 3½ in) rectangles. Stick an invisible mount to the two left-hand back corners of each rectangle.

5 Stick the paper to the back of the card, butting the left-hand edge up to the spine and positioning it centrally top to bottom. Here the text is positioned so that only the '40' shows in the aperture.

40
40

christmas gift

materials

spotted embossed wallpaper

thick card

paper adhesive

craft knife

steel rule

cutting mat

narrow silver ribbon

scissors

double-sided tape

12 x 17cm (4¾ x 6¾ in) smooth white card blank

glue pen

sequins

techniques

double-sided tape, *page 13*

adhesives, *page 16*

embossed wallpaper, *page 86*

Like all projects where large quantities are involved, it's best to set up a mini production line; preparing the squares, tying the ribbons, sticking the motifs to the cards, and so on. Best of all, split the tasks between the family and have a jolly evening getting into the festive spirit.

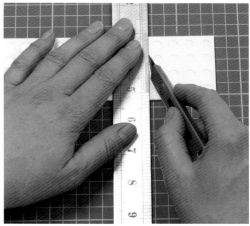

1 Cut a 5cm (2½ in) strip of wallpaper, taking the placing of the pattern into account. Using paper adhesive, stick the wallpaper to an identically sized piece of the thick card.

2 Using the craft knife and steel rule on the cutting mat, cut the strip into 5cm (2½ in) squares.

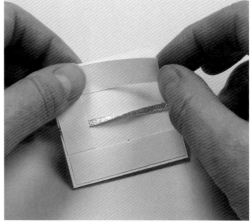

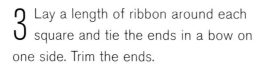

3 Lay a length of ribbon around each square and tie the ends in a bow on one side. Trim the ends.

4 Working on the back, stick double-sided tape around the edges of the square. Peel off the backing.

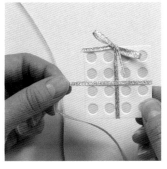

5 Lay a piece of ribbon across the square at right angles to the first piece. Stick the ends to the tape on the back.

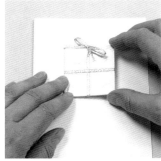

6 Stick the whole square to the front of the card.

7 Embellish the square further by using a glue pen to stick on a few sequins.

halloween party

This project incorporates a number of different techniques so it is best suited to smaller batch runs – perhaps four or eight – as an unusual party invitation, or maybe as a card for special friends. If you have time, decorate the envelopes with ink-blot spiders.

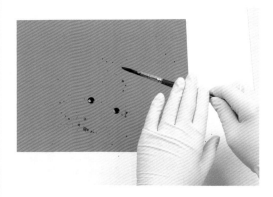

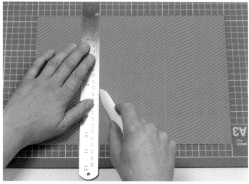

1 Lay the sheet of orange card on some scrap paper. Using the paintbrush, splatter a little black ink over it. Leave it to dry.

2 Using the bone folder and steel rule, score two lines on the back of the card at 10cm (4in) intervals, to divide it into three equal sections.

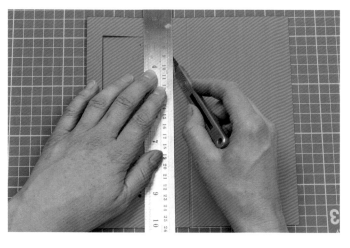

3 Fold the right-hand section of the card into the middle, folding it on the scored line. Open it out flat again and, using the craft knife and steel rule on the cutting mat, cut 2mm (1/16 in) off the right-hand edge.

4 Fold the right-hand section back in again. Mark a 9 x 7cm (3½ x 2¾ in) aperture on the back of this section, 2cm (¾ in) down from the top edge and centred on the width. Using the craft knife and steel rule on the cutting mat, cut out the aperture, cutting through both layers of card.

5 Open the card out flat. On the back of the card, stick lengths of double-sided tape around the edges of both apertures and around the outer edges of the flap.

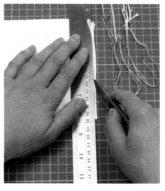

6 Fold the white polythene bags up together and, using the craft knife and steel rule on the cutting mat, cut them into narrow strips.

7 Lay the clear polythene flat on a sheet of greaseproof paper. Lay eight of the strips of white polythene on it in a star shape.

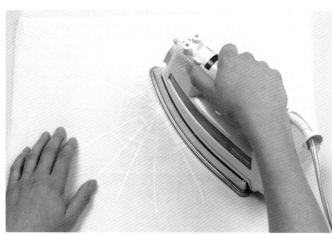

8 Coil more strips of white polythene round on top of the star to make a web, overlapping the ends of the strips as necessary. The web must be large enough for one quarter to fill the aperture in the orange card (this means that one web will make four cards).

9 Lay the sheet of greaseproof paper over the web and iron it gently with a warm iron. You do not need a second layer of polythene.

10 Using the craft knife and steel rule on the cutting mat, cut each web into quarters.

11 Peel the paper backing off the tape on the middle panel of the card. Stick a section of web over the aperture. Peel the tape off the flap and stick it down. Fold the card along the second score line.

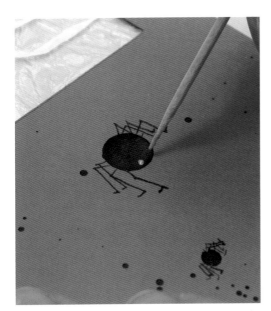

12 Turn some of the larger spots of black ink into spiders by drawing legs on them with the fine, black felt-tipped pen. Make eyes by dabbing on tiny dots of three-dimensional paint with the tip of a cocktail stick.

13 Stick a spider sticker to the web. If you are using small plastic spiders, stick them on with a dab of all-purpose glue.

finger-print mice

materials

12 x 9cm
(4¾ x 3½in)
pre-scored white
card blanks

craft knife

steel rule

cutting mat

fawn ink pad

pale pink stencil paint

pencil with eraser
on the end

darning needle

pale pink double
knitting yarn

scissors

techniques

printing with
found objects,
page 25

hand stitching,
page 36

Especially quick and easy to make, this card is well suited to batch production. It would make a lovely child's party invitation and children will enjoy being involved in the printing process. Alternatively, use the idea to create very sweet birth announcement cards.

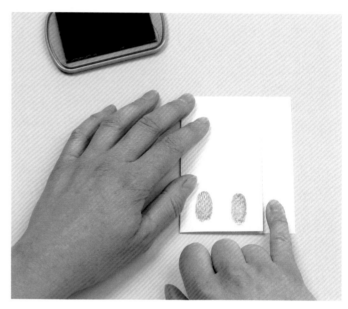

1 Using the craft knife and steel rule on the cutting mat, cut 2.5cm (1in) off the front leading edge of the card.

2 Dab your forefinger-tip onto the ink pad and make a finger print on the front of the card, close to the fold and the bottom edge. Do the same with your index finger, printing next to the first print. Print again with your little fingertip, printing on the inside back of the card revealed by the cut-away front edge.

3 Spread a little pink paint out on a plate. Dip the eraser into it and stamp ears at the tops of the fingerprint-mice bodies. Leave to dry.

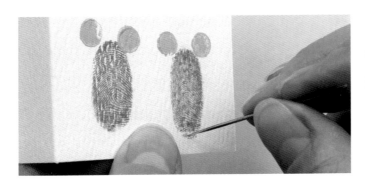

4 Pierce a hole with the darning needle at the bottom of each body.

5 Tie a knot in the end of a length of yarn. Push the needle through a hole from the back and pull the yarn through up to the knot. Repeat the process to give each mouse a tail.

6 Stand the card up so that the tails lie flat in front of it. Trim the tails to different lengths.

wedding invitation

materials

computer

colour printer

thin white card

steel rule

cutting mat

circular aperture
punch

organza ribbon

self-adhesive pads

12cm (4¾ in) square
white textured
card blanks

silver heart sequins

scissors

Create unique and personal wedding invitations for your special day.
The techniques used mean it is feasible to make a large number of
cards in the wedding colour scheme. The idea could easily be
adapted to make other wedding stationery, such as place cards.

techniques

self-adhesive pads,
page 18

punching apertures,
page 22

1 Print out the couple's name on the thin white card.
The names should be spaced so that they fit into
a rectangle 9.5cm (3¾ in) wide and 6cm (2¼ in)
deep, with the names themselves close to the right-
hand side. Trim to 9.5cm- (3¾ in-) wide strips. Using
the steel rule, tear the card into 6cm- (2¼ in-) deep
strips. Use the marks on the cutting mat to guide you.

2 Punch a round
aperture in the left-
hand side of each
rectangle of printed card.

3 Cut a length of ribbon
and fold the length in
half. Push the loop
through the aperture
from the back. Tuck the
free ends of the ribbon
through the loop and pull
it tight. If you are using
wide ribbon, twist it a few
times before folding it in
half so that the loop sits
neatly on the card.

4 Stick a self-adhesive pad to each corner of the back of each rectangle. Stick each rectangle to the front of a card, positioning it 2cm (³⁄₄ in) down from the top edge, with the right hand sides aligned.

5 Stick a small self-adhesive pad to the back of a heart sequin. Stick the sequin inside the circular aperture.

6 Trim the ends of the ribbon at an angle.

colourful flowers

The larger the sheet of paper, the more background you can decorate in one go; position the stamped strips to make the most of the background pattern on each card. These cards would make lovely invitations to a summer lunch or garden party.

1 Decorate the mediumweight watercolour paper by wetting it with a foam brush and then dripping on the magenta ink first, followed by the burnt sienna ink.

2 Allow the paper to absorb the water for a few minutes, then drip a little more magenta ink on to it.

3 Flick some clean water over the whole sheet of paper to soften and blend the ink colours. Leave to dry.

4 Trim the edges off the paper, as the inks may have marked the back of it. Cut the paper into 26 x 13cm (10 x 5in) rectangles.

5 Draw a light pencil line 0.5cm (¼ in) down from the top of the sheet of lightweight watercolour paper. Draw more lines every 4cm (1½ in) until you have one for each rectangle cut in Step 4. Leave 0.5cm (¼ in) of paper below the last line.

6 Make a punched rubber stamp using a flower punch. Stick it to a bottle top.

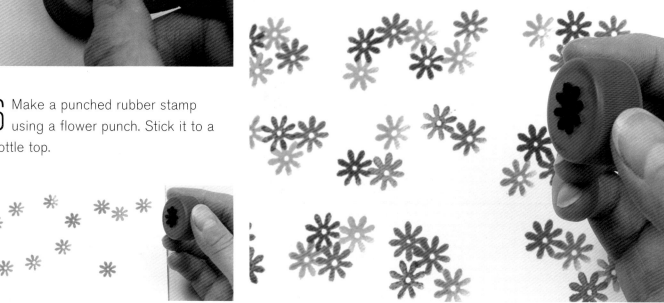

7 Stamp orange flowers along each marked-out strip of paper.

8 Stamp vermillion flowers on each strip, allowing some to overlap the orange flowers. Repeat the process with the garnet ink pad. Leave some areas blank for punching.

9 Lay the steel rule along each pencil line in turn and tear the stamped paper into strips.

10 Punch flowers in the blank areas. Use the leather punch to punch small holes in the centre of some of the stamped flowers.

11 Spray glue on the back of each punched strip and stick them to the decorated rectangles. Position the front edge 4cm (1½ in) from the leading edge of the card – use the marks on the cutting mat to guide you.

12 Score the card down the middle on the inside. Fold it carefully in half. As the inked paper can buckle a little while being decorated, it is a good idea to keep the cards flat under a heavy book overnight.

christmas tree

materials

black felt-tipped pen

fine-textured
bath sponge

bread knife

cutting mat

dark green
acrylic paint

plate

paintbrush

15 x 10cm (6 x 4in)
white card blanks

steel rule

bone folder

craft knife

leather punch

silver star sequins

self-adhesive pads

If you want to make your own Christmas cards but are put off by the quantity needed, this project is the solution. Set up a mini production line, so all the stamping is done first, followed by cutting and folding and finally all the detailing. Make the stamp to fit the cards.

1 Using the felt-tipped pen, draw a triangle on the bath sponge. Using the bread knife, cut out the shape. Cut carefully to keep the edges straight, and never cut towards your hand.

2 Spread some paint onto the plate. Using the paintbrush, brush green paint onto the surface of the sponge. Brush the paint on quite thickly.

techniques

folding a card,
page 12

self-adhesive pads,
page 18

punching shapes,
page 20

stamping,
page 29

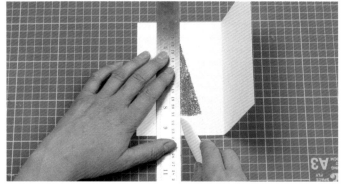

3 Stamp the triangle onto the inside front of the card. The triangle must be centred on the card front for the design to work. Leave to dry.

4 Lay the rule down the middle of the tree. Score lines down the card from the top to the tip of the tree, and from halfway across the base of the tree to the bottom of the card. (The line must be parallel to the leading edge of the card, so ensure that the top line touches the tip of the tree, but if the bottom line isn't exactly halfway across the base, it doesn't matter.)

5 Using the craft knife on the cutting mat, cut from the scored line at the top of the tree, down the right-hand side, and across the bottom to the scored line at the base of the tree. Cut just beyond the green edge so that the tree has a white border. If you are not confident about cutting freehand, use a steel rule to cut against.

6 Fold the front of the card back on itself, folding it on the scored lines so that the tree comes to the front.

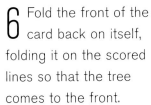

7 Punch some small holes randomly within the tree shape.

8 Stick a self-adhesive pad to the back of a sequin and stick it to the top of the tree.

change of address

Ensure your special friends never lose your new address by sending them a card they will want to keep. If time is short, you could simplify the design a little using brown parcel paper alone as a background and a rubber stamp to decorate the luggage tag.

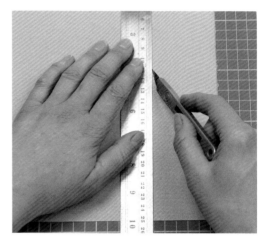

1 Lay the steel rule 0.5cm (¼ in) from the right-hand edge of the sheet of ridged paper. Tear along the edge of the rule.

2 Measure 6cm (2½ in) from the torn edge. Using the steel rule and craft knife on the cutting mat, cut a 6cm- (2½ in-) wide strip of ridged paper. Repeat the process until you have as many strips as needed.

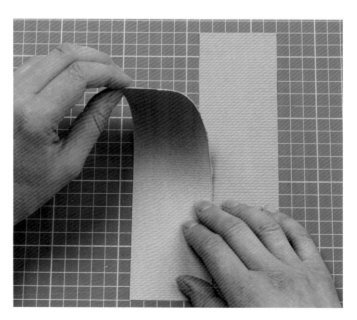

3 Stick a length of double-sided tape to the back of the torn edge. Peel off the paper backing and stick the ridged paper to the left-hand edge of a parcel paper strip. The ridged paper should overlap the parcel paper by 1cm (½ in), so use the markings on a cutting mat to guide you.

4 Make a rubber stamp of your new house number. Stick it onto a piece of translucent plastic, so that you can easily see where you are stamping.

5 Stamp the number onto the ridged paper, starting approximately 1cm (½ in) from the top edge. Space the stamps approximately 4.5cm (1¾ in) apart. Re-ink the stamp every second or third time, to produce stamped numbers of different densities. Leave to dry.

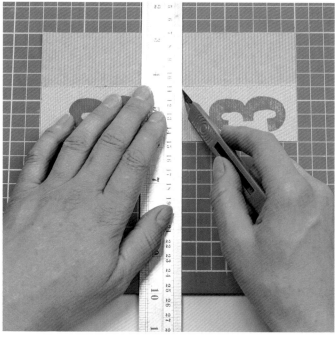

6 Position one of the printed numbers in a card aperture. When it is as you would like it, measure and mark with pencil dots the position of the papers within the aperture.

7 Using the steel rule and craft knife, cut as many squares of paper as you need, positioning the number on each one as in Step 6.

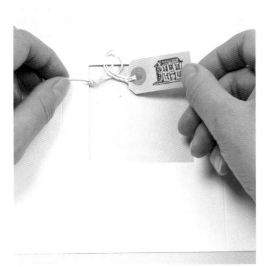

8 Punch a small hole above the top edge of the aperture, close to the left-hand corner. Stick narrow double-sided tape around the edges of the aperture, ensuring that you don't cover the punched hole.

9 Use thinners to transfer an image of a house onto as many luggage tags as needed.

10 Working from back to front, push both ends of the luggage tag string through the hole. Tie them together in a knot, then push the tag through the loop.

11 Peel the paper backing off the tape. Position the aperture over a square of numbered paper and stick it down. Use double-sided tape to stick down the flap that covers the back of the aperture.

12 Stick a self-adhesive pad to the back of the luggage tag and stick it to the front of the card, overlapping the edge of the aperture a little.

party invitation

A sophisticated card where light and shadow create the effect, this project would be suitable for making elegant invitations to a grown-up dinner party. You can have fun arranging the simple components in a different way on each card. Subtle texture provides further interest.

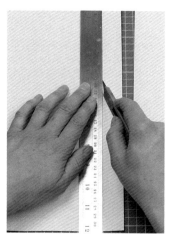

1 Spray a sheet of thin card with fleckstone spray paint, following the manufacturer's instructions. Leave to dry.

2 Using the craft knife and steel rule on the cutting mat, cut the sprayed card into strips. Cut some strips 5cm (2in) wide and some 2.5cm (1in) wide.

3 Cut the 5cm (2in) strips into 5cm (2in) squares. Cut the 2.5cm (1in) strips into a selection of 2.5cm (1in) squares and 4cm (1½ in) rectangles.

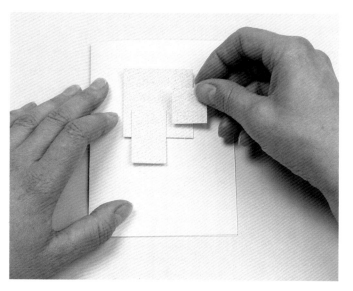

4 Arrange a large square, a small square and a rectangle on the front of a card. When you are happy with the arrangement, take the elements off the card and stick them together with self-adhesive pads.

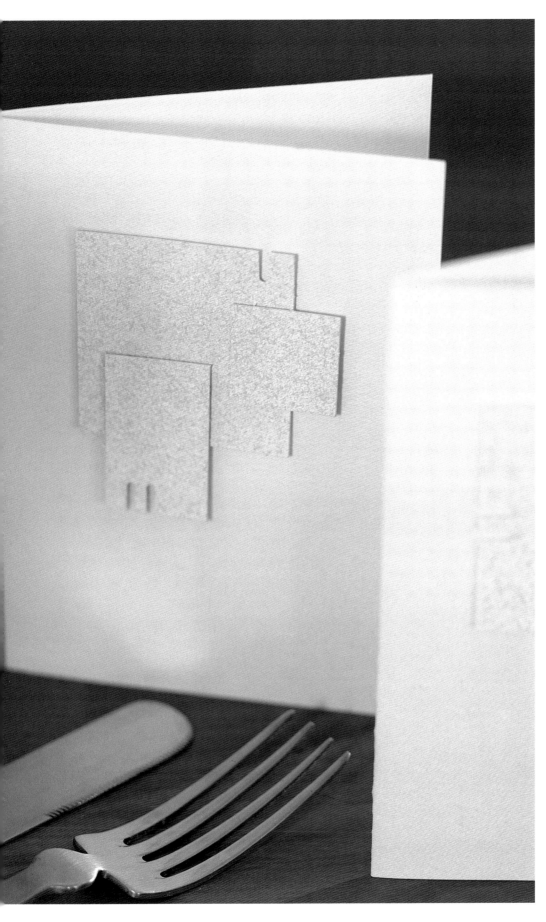

5 Use a slot punch to punch holes in the edges of some elements.

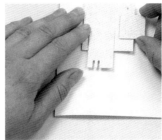

6 Stick the panel to the front of the card with self-adhesive pads. Stick it so that the top part of the panel is 2.5cm (1in) from the top of the card. This gives a uniformity to the cards, despite the different arrangements.

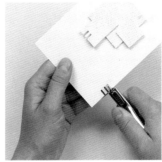

7 Punch some slots in the edges of the card itself.

templates

To transfer any of the templates in this section onto a card, first use tracing paper to trace them off from the page. With the tracing face-down and using a soft pencil, scribble over the back of the traced lines. Lay the template in position on the card and draw firmly over the traced lines. If the lines are very faint, you can draw over them again in pencil before starting work.

If you only need the outline shape, you can photocopy or trace the template and cut it out to make a pattern. Lay the template in position on the card and cut around it, or draw around it in pencil to transfer the outline.

Template for **simple shaped card**
(page 32). Use at full size.

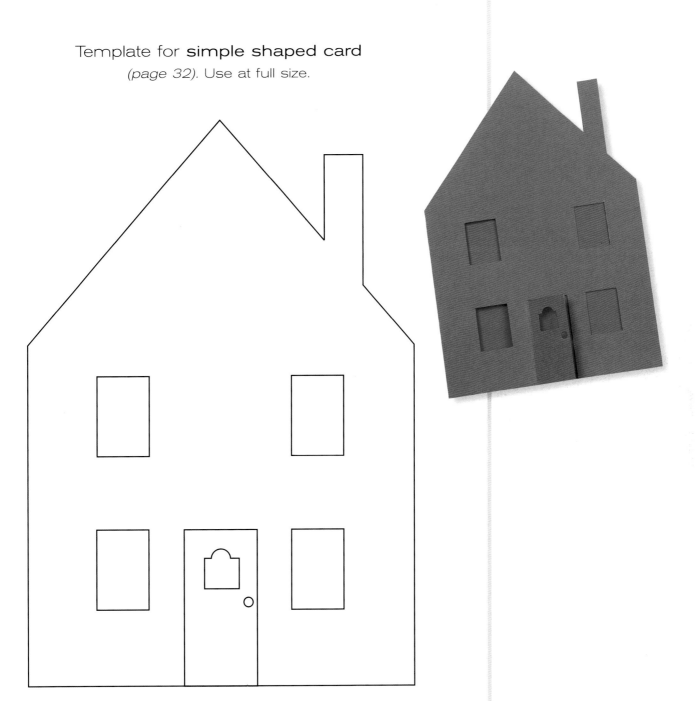

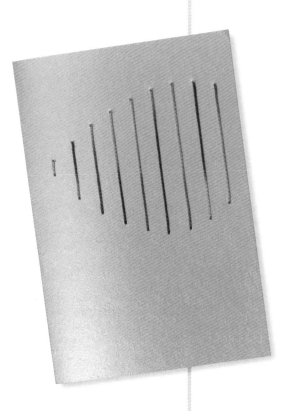

Template for **hand-stitching**
(page 36). Use at full size.

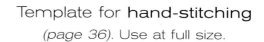

Template for **kitchen foil**
(page 40). Use at full size.

Template for **baking parchment**

(page 42). Use at full size.

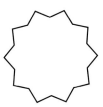

Template for **pieces from the scrapbag**

(page 48). Use at full size.

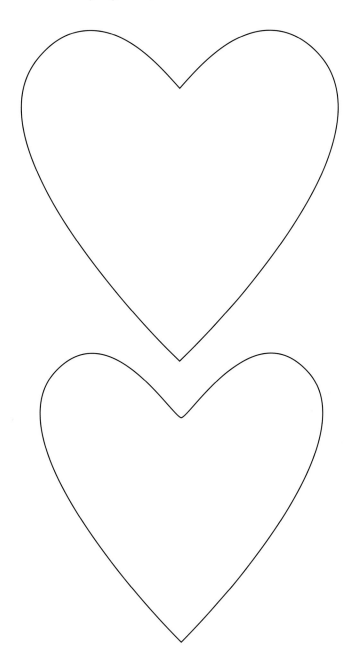

Template for **colourful christmas**
(page 58). Use at full size.

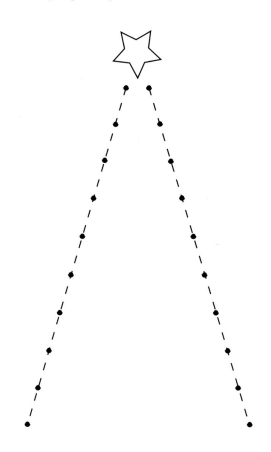

Template for **flowerpot**
(page 72). Use at full size.

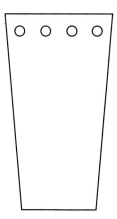

acknowledgements

My thanks to all who made *Fast Cards* a reality, especially to Marie Clayton at Collins & Brown for commissioning this book while *The Complete Guide to Card Making* was still largely an untested work. To my editor, Kate Haxell, and to Matthew Dickens for the photography; I really enjoyed working with you both and I hope that we can look forward to future projects together. To Justina Leitão for designing the book. Last, but especially not least, a big thank you to my family and friends for constant love, support, interest and encouragement.

The motif for *Kitchen foil* (page 40) was taken from *The Glass Painter's Motif Library* by Alan D Gear and Barry L Freestone. (Collins & Brown).

suppliers

Sarah Beaman produces a range of card-making kits; more information can be found at sarahbeaman.com

UK

Celestial
Retailers of designer buttons and trimmings.
162 Archway Road
London N6 5BB
Tel: 020 8341 2788

Craft Creations
Greetings cards blanks and accessories.
Mail-order service.
Ingersoll House
Delamare Road, Cheshunt
Hertfordshire EN8 9HD
Tel: 01992 781 900
Email: enquiries@craftcreations.com
Web: www.craftcreations.com

The Cutting Edge
A large range of ready-made card blanks, paper and envelopes that are recycled or sourced from 'greener' manufacturers. Also a growing range of equipment and materials including rubber stamps, paper punches, craft knives and decorative-edge scissors.
Unit 17a, C.E.C.
Mill Lane, Coppull
Lancashire PR7 5BW
Tel: 01257 792025
Email: enquiries@eco-craft.co.uk
Web: www.eco-craft.co.uk

Hobbycraft
Art and craft superstores.
Tel: 0800 0272387 for your nearest branch

Stampeezee
Specialists in card-making materials.
349 Walsgrave Road
Ball Hill
Coventry CV2 4BE
Tel: 024 7644 8085
email: stampeezee@hotmail.com

Lakeland Limited
A range of craft materials and equipment.
Tel: 015394 88100 for your nearest branch or a catalogue.

In addition the following wholesale suppliers distribute quality materials, some of which have been used in this book, to many art and craft stores across the country. Do ask about their products in your local craft store.

Robert Horne Paper
A range of interesting papers.

R.K.Burt & Company Ltd
A wide range of specialist papers, quality card blanks and stationery.

USA

Kate's Paperie
Retailers of all types of paper and card blanks.
561 Broadway
New York, NY 10012
Tel: 888 941 9169
Web: www.katespaperie.com

Swallow Creek Papers
Retailers of fine papers.
PO Box 152
Spring Mills, PA 16875
Tel: 814 422 8651

Flax Art & Design
Papers and card-making equipment.
1699 Market Street
San Francisco, CA 94103
Tel: 415 552 2355
Web: www.flaxart.com

Michaels
Art and craft materials of all kinds.
Tel: 800 642 4235
Web: www.michaels.com

index